LOVE AND DUTY

LOVE AND DUTY

BEN AND ANNE PURCELL

ST. MARTIN'S PRESS   NEW YORK

Editor: Jared Kieling
Production Editor: Eric C. Meyer
Design by Dawn Niles

Library of Congress Cataloging-in-Publication Data

Purcell, Ben.
Love and duty / Ben and Anne Purcell.
p. cm.
ISBN 0-312-07020-9
1. Vietnamese Conflict, 1961–1975—Missing in action—United States. 2. Purcell, Ben. 3. Purcell, Anne. I. Purcell, Anne.
II. Title.
DS559.8.M5P87   1992
959.704'37—dc20   91-33187
[B]   CIP

First Edition: February 1992

10 9 8 7 6 5 4 3 2 1

DEDICATED TO THE MEMORY OF:

Clarice Ann Purcell, whose memory lives within our hearts.

S. Sgt. James E. George, a soldier who gave his life that others might taste the fruits of freedom.

Those American servicemen who remain missing in action on battlefields throughout our nation's history.

CONTENTS

ACKNOWLEDGMENTS

Our deepest thanks and appreciation to:

Ms. Linda Hamm Lucas for her encouragement, which prompted us to begin to write this book.

Mr. Robert Vaughan for his sage advice, professional assistance, and personal friendship, without which this book would never have been published.

To David, Debbie, Clifford, Sherri, and Joy, who lived the experience with us and whose very presence provided a bottomless reservoir of strength throughout our ordeal.

To our many friends and loved ones who took the time to read the first drafts of the manuscript and share with us their comments, and to our daughter-in-law, Lisa, who spent so many hours typing and duplicating the manuscript.

FOREWORD

Love and Duty is a powerful book, not because of its scope, but because of the depth of the unique experience of one man and the trauma suffered by his wife and family.

The war in Vietnam was a new experience for the American people in many ways. Our national objectives were limited, the employment of our power was restrained, and public support was shallow. But the demands upon the men and women of our military services—especially those on the battlefield—were very real and profound. The account of those special American citizens has been covered in many books. But the story of our men held captive by the enemy and the trauma of their families has been minimal.

At last, that story is told by Colonel Purcell and his wife, Anne. Colonel Purcell, a career army officer, was held captive by the North Vietnamese Communist enemy for five long years. His wife and five children did not know whether he was dead or alive.

This book is an account of dedication, courage, and resourcefulness and a story of devotion to God, family, country and love in every sense of the word.

William C. Westmoreland
General U.S. Army (Retired)

PROLOGUE

ANNE'S STORY

I thought that if I left them there, I could wake up one day and none of this would have happened.

But they were there, in the garage, next to the washer and dryer, and when I got in or out of the car, I would see them. When I did the wash I would see them, and if I looked out the kitchen door to see if the kids were coming home, or even just to check if it was raining . . . I would see them.

On the surface there wasn't anything particularly intimidating about them. They were two footlockers, made of plywood and painted with the army's olive drab. A name was printed on the lid in the (to a military wife) familiar, disconnected lettering left by a stencil:

PURCELL, B.H. LIEUTENANT COLONEL
U.S. ARMY 061035

Finally I knew I could put it off no longer. One rainy morning after the kids had gone to school I fortified myself with a cup of coffee and dragged the two footlockers into the house. I sat on the floor in the living room and went through

Ben's things. Everything in these two boxes had been packed very carefully for shipment back to the next of kin. Who were the soldiers who put the things in these crates? Did they know what they were touching, what I would feel as I withdrew each item?

Did they know, for example, about the foam-rubber pillow? It was Ben's special pillow; he said he couldn't sleep without it, and he had taken it to Vietnam with him. Before that it had been on the bed at home . . . our bed. The bed had been so empty since he had left. And now that the pillow was here without him, that emptiness was magnified a hundredfold.

I continued to unpack his things, and as I did disconnected, irrational thoughts tumbled through my mind.

Why did they send me his extra pair of boots? He'll be needing these boots.

There is his tape recorder . . . no . . . that shouldn't be here. How can he play my tapes without this?

The pictures . . . surely he'll want the pictures.

I took the uniforms out and put them on hangers. The greens looked as if they were ready for him to wear. The crossed rifles and U.S. pins on the lapels shined as brightly as if Ben had just buffed them with Brasso. The service ribbons, row on row, and the Combat Infantryman's Badge were neatly in place. This uniform was so much a part of my life with Ben that I kept expecting him to walk out of the other room within the next minute, wrapped in a towel, his hair still damp from a shower, asking me if his uniform was ready to put on.

But he wouldn't be coming out of the other room in the next minute, the next month, or the next year. He was missing in action, status unknown. I knew that these boxes might be all I would ever have of him.

I held the uniform jacket to my face. It almost seemed as if I could smell his after-shave—an illusory impression I'm sure, but the sensation was there. For this one bittersweet moment, I could feel him with me. I didn't want to let go of the moment . . . yet the pain of it was almost more than I could bear.

BEN'S STORY

I was having a very difficult time with depression. I reasoned with myself that depression was normal under my circumstances. After all, I was a prisoner of war, I was malnourished, I was in total isolation, and I had no idea when this ordeal would end or even if it would end.

I was also depressed because I couldn't shake the nagging feeling that I had somehow done less than my full measure of duty. I was a soldier. It was my duty to avoid capture. If I was captured, it then became my duty to escape. Or at least . . . to attempt to escape.

From the moment I began seriously considering escape as a possibility my mood improved. And with my mind freed from the melancholy of my condition, I was able to begin conceiving a legitimate escape plan.

Coming back from emptying my toilet bucket one day, I happened to notice the lock on my cell door. It reminded me of the kind of lock one might have found on a barn door a century ago. It was an old iron padlock with a large keyhole. There was a pin in the middle of the keyhole, so the key that was used had to be hollow. There was no chance of stealing the key so I was going to have to make one.

Without the real key to use or copy, or to even make an impression from, it would be extremely difficult. I was going to have to determine, by some other means, the dimensions and unique characteristics of my key.

But suppose I was able to open the door . . . what would I do next? I was in an enemy prison camp in the middle of the enemy's country. I remembered from the long trek up here from where I was captured that it would be a hike of several hundred miles in any direction before I could expect to reach friendly hands.

Studying the layout of the camp, I determined a possible escape route. Across the compound from my cell was a cistern. The top of the cistern could be reached by a set of steps and from there it would be an easy jump across to the roof of the rearmost building. That building butted up against the compound wall, so anyone sliding down the other side of the roof would be able to drop off onto the street outside the prison walls. After getting over the wall, I would proceed northward until I reached the Red River.

Beyond that my plan was to take the toilet bucket, empty it, and then, using scrap pieces of cloth, tie the lid tightly shut to make a buoy. By turning the bucket upside down and holding onto its handle, I would float down the Red River to Haiphong Harbor. Once I made it through the harbor and out into the open sea there was no doubt in my mind that the U.S. Navy would soon find me and pick me up.

But none of that would matter if I couldn't get out of my cell, and for that I needed to make the key. There was a sliding panel on the door through which the guards could keep us under observation. By opening that panel as wide as it would go, I could stick my arm out and reach the padlock keyhole. I couldn't do that, of course, with the guards watching, so I needed a period of time when I knew I wouldn't be observed. By studying the habits of the guard I learned that his routine never varied. From the time he passed my cell door I would have approximately thirty minutes until I saw him again.

The first thing I had to determine was the outside diameter of the keyhole. I did this by making a roll of paper a little smaller in diameter than a cigarette. Using one of the periods when I knew I couldn't be seen, and with the panel pushed open, I stuck my arm through the hole and tried to insert the roll of paper into the keyhole. The roll of paper was too large, so I tore off a couple of layers and tried again. When it fit the diameter of the keyhole, I had the outside dimensions. I reinserted the roll farther into the keyhole, and when I withdrew it and counted the number of layers of paper the pin had displaced, I was able to ascertain the diameter of the pin.

Next, I needed to learn the number of tumblers and their size and location. In order to do this I fashioned a tight roll from the thin aluminum of an empty toothpaste tube. Near the end of the roll I cut the aluminum so I could raise a piece of it about as wide as the lock was deep and then cut this flange into a series of slices, or "fingers." My idea was to insert this aluminum tube into the keyhole, turn it slowly, and then withdraw it and look at the fingers. The fingers would have been bent by the tumblers. In this way I would have a "negative" or template of the interior of the lock.

Once I had the diameter of the hole and pin and the location, number, and size of the tumblers, I was ready to begin making a key.

I needed something long, round, hard, and hollow. I found the perfect medium for that in one of the rib bones from the dog meat we were occasionally served in our soup. By shaping the outside of the bone and scraping the marrow from the inside, I was able to construct the shaft of the key. Next I had to have the key tangs, which would trip the tumblers. To make the tangs I used very stiff pieces of wire that I had removed from a broken neon light bulb I found at the wash place. I then forced the tangs into holes drilled at precise locations near the end of the bone sheath.

To make the key I had to take "readings," make adjustments, and then take more readings of the inside of the lock. Then one night, three weeks after I had begun work, I saw the guard pass by on his routine round. As soon as he disappeared around the corner I pushed the panel all the way open and reached outside to make what was, by then, my twenty-second adjustment. Suddenly I found myself face to face with an angry guard! This wasn't the regular guard, and he wasn't following the routine I had so carefully plotted. On the eve of success, my escape plot was foiled.

I felt a sense of frustration and disappointment . . . but not despair and certainly not depression. I knew now that a serious escape plot could be formulated and carried out. And I intended to try again.

But I am getting ahead of my story.

I

A CALL TO ARMS

BEN'S STORY

In May of 1945 I graduated from high school in the small northeastern Georgia town of Clarkesville. The war in Europe had just ended, but the battles continued to rage in the Pacific theater of operations. For several years I had stood by as my older brother, Vernon, and many of my friends had left Clarkesville for military service. I wanted to do my part for the war effort, for it was the only honorable thing to do in those days, so I joined the U.S. Navy.

After ten months of service I was released from active duty and returned home. In March 1947, I enrolled at North Georgia College, a small military college located in Dahlonega, Georgia.

During orientation week at NGC in the fall of 1949, I met a beautiful girl. By this time I was a senior and a cadet officer in the corps, and she was a freshman. Her name was Anne Grant, and she was from Baldwin, Georgia, a town only ten miles from Clarkesville.

I noticed her name on the barrette in her blond hair and said, "Anne, the next time we meet I want you to speak to me." She answered "Yes, sir," somewhat surprised that I knew her name and even more surprised that a senior cadet would take notice of her presence. We began dating soon after that and eventually fell deeply in love.

On the fifteenth of March, 1950, I received my Bachelor of Science degree in physics and simultaneously was commissioned a second lieutenant, Regular Army, Infantry Branch. I began my active duty as an army lieutenant at Fort Riley, Kansas, but when the Korean War broke out, I was transferred to Fort Jackson, South Carolina to assist in reopening that post, which was closed following World War II.

Every weekend during the fall of 1950 I traveled the two hundred miles to Baldwin to visit Anne. We committed our lives to each other and were married on January 20, 1951. At that time Anne thought she was aware of most of the problems associated with being an army wife, but she was soon to learn the real sacrifices wives of career servicemen have to endure. Within three weeks I received orders for duty in Korea. Anne, left alone, returned to North Georgia College to continue her education.

In early December of 1951 while my battalion was defending Heartbreak Ridge, I received an order to report to regimental headquarters for an interview as a prospective junior aide-de-camp to General W. B. Palmer, the newly arrived commander of Tenth Corps. I was selected.

On the morning of December 14 General Palmer was making a flying tour of his area, and I was to follow him in a second aircraft. Captain Stuart McCash, the senior aide-de-camp, came into the office and told me to "stay back" and take over the duty of running the office, saying he would take over the duty of field aide. An hour later our corps chief of staff received a call from General Palmer stating that the L-19 aircraft that was carrying Captain McCash had had a mid-air collision with an air force observation plane and had crashed. Stuart McCash, who only one hour before had voluntarily taken my place, was dead.

On the eighteenth of December, 1951, General Palmer accepted Major Hugh Casey as his new senior aide. When Major Casey arrived from duty in another corps, he wanted to spend some time in the Tenth Corps G-3 shop becoming familiar with the order of battle, the location of subordinate units, and so forth. I continued to go to the field with General Palmer daily and was scheduled to go with him again on the eleventh of January, 1952. But Major Casey came into the tent that morning and said, "Ben, I'll fly with the 'old man' today. You stay back and take care of the office and the compound." Within two hours we received word that Major Casey's L-19 had crashed into a mountain and that he had died on the way to the hospital. For the second time in less than thirty days an officer who had volunteered to take my place had been killed. General Palmer was devastated and did not get another senior aide for two months.

When I returned from Korea in May 1952 Anne met me at the Atlanta airport driving a new car, our first. She was also sporting a new hairdo. I hardly recognized her, but that fact didn't hamper in the least our second honeymoon.

In the summer of 1953 I was selected to attend the U.S. Naval Post Graduate School, located in Monterey, California, to study nuclear engineering. Anne was seven months pregnant with our first child and had a tough time as we traveled to California through Arizona in the 115-degree heat.

On October 24, 1953, Anne's father, Nace Grant, passed away in Georgia, but she couldn't attend the funeral because of her pregnancy. Three days later our first child was born in the army hospital at Ford Ord, California. We named him David Nace after his grandfather.

In the fall of 1955 our second child, Clarice Ann, was born in the army hospital at Fort McClellan, Alabama. I had been detailed to duty with the Chemical Corps and for two years served as radiological safety control officer for our nuclear testing program in Nevada and the Pacific. From there I went to Fort Benning, Georgia, where our third child, Debora Lynne, was born in May 1957. That summer Clarice became ill from a mysterious disease. After three weeks of extensive medical tests in Martin Army Hospital at Fort Benning, she was diagnosed as having rheumatoid arthritis. We were worried about her health but were convinced the army doctors could control the illness.

In June 1959 I was transferred to France and assigned to the U.S. Communications Zone, Europe. Anne had been denied concurrent travel due to shortage of housing, so she remained in Columbus, Georgia, to await orders to follow. The very day I was assigned a set of quarters in France, Clarice had a serious setback and was rehospitalized at Fort Benning. Anne had to put her move to France on hold until Clarice was released.

By late August 1959 Anne had orders to travel. She supervised the packing of household goods, sold our car, obtained passports and other travel documents, and flew to France. Despite having three young children and being seven months pregnant, Anne succeeded in getting to France.

On November 4, 1959, Clarice was admitted to the U.S. Armed Forces Hospital at La Chappelle, France, located on the outskirts of Orleans. On November 9 Anne gave birth to our fourth child, Clifford Alan. On November 21 Clarice went into a coma, and despite the best efforts of many doctors, she died. Our life was dealt a severe blow. Anne remained in France with our three children while I made the sad journey to take Clarice's body back to Georgia for burial.

After three years in France I was selected to attend the U.S. Command and General Staff College at Fort Leavenworth, Kansas. We arrived in early August 1962, and another daughter, Sherri Denise, was born on September 7.

Upon completion of the command and general staff course in June 1963, I was assigned as the professor of military science at Kemper Military School and College in Boonville, Missouri. This was a great assignment. I was able to perform my military service in a fine educational institution, while at the same time Anne and the children had all the benefits of living in a civilian community. We became very close to members of the staff and faculty of Kemper as well as to fellow members of the Boonville Baptist Church.

My assignment as PMS at Kemper was extended from the normal three years to four, and it was there in Boonville in December of 1965 that our daughter Joy Renee was born.

By early spring of 1967 I felt a strong need professionally to get back into regular army assignments. After talking the matter over with Anne, I volunteered for duty in Vietnam.

Throughout all our years together Anne had never complained about her role as a faithful and loyal wife. She is a

loving and gentle person but "tough as nails" when necessary—the perfect army wife and mother. I had no doubt that
she could handle the situation during my absence.

On August 27 Anne and I gathered the children around
us in the living room of our home at 715 Pendleton Avenue
for a family discussion about the upcoming thirteen months
of separation and for a family prayer.

Three hours later, at the airport in Kansas City, I told
the family good-bye.

In Vietnam I was assigned as deputy commander of the
Da Nang Sub-Area Command and concurrently as the executive officer of the 80th General Support Group, a subordinate
unit of the First Logistic Command. Our area of responsibility
was I Corps, which was made up of the northern five prov-
inces of South Vietnam and extended approximately 120
miles north and south of our headquarters in Da Nang.* Initially our unit was busy keeping the First and Third Marine
Divisions resupplied with ammunition and repair parts for the
army weapons utilized by the marines, specifically the 240
MM guns and the 155 MM self-propelled howitzers.

During the fall of 1967 and early 1968 our mission ex-
panded as the marine divisions were joined by the army's
American Division, the First Calvary Division (Airmobile),
and elements of the 101st Airborne Division. In order to visit
all of our units supporting this larger force I frequently traveled by aircraft and helicopter.

At Da Nang I enjoyed many more amenities than I had
reason to expect in a combat zone. But then the Vietnam
conflict was not an ordinary war.

I lived in a newly constructed BOQ, or bachelor officers
quarters. My two-room suite had a private bath with hot and
cold water and even an air conditioner. The dining hall was
very close to the BOQ and the meals were super—ice cream
every day and steak at least once a week.

---

*The "I" is Roman numeral one. In conversation it was generally referred to as
First Corps. South Vietnam was divided into three regions, or corps, to facilitate
command and control of military forces. Within each corps there was a Vietnamese and a U.S. command structure for respective forces. In I Corps the U.S. command structure in early 1968 was the Third Marine Amphibious Force (3rd MAF).

We had a good place to work and outstanding officers and soldiers to work with. My commander, Colonel John Pierce, was very demanding, but his forceful leadership brought out the very best in our men. I also became close friends with Chaplain (Major) Bill Bagnal and did whatever I could to help him as he ministered to our troops at the Chapel of Flags. The chapel was appropriately named because Bill had obtained a flag from each state and had suspended them from the rafters along each wall. This small touch of home provided each soldier with a sense of belonging to our unit.

Finally, I was in touch with Anne daily by letter, weekly by audiotape, and monthly by telephone. In sum, I had a busy and relatively secure life with all personal and professional needs fulfilled.

Little did I suspect that soon this situation would change drastically and that I would begin a long struggle for food, water, and even life.

2

SHOOTDOWN

At midnight on Tuesday, January 30, 1968, the Vietnamese were celebrating Tet, their new year. It was the "Year of the Monkey."

When I try to explain Tet to Americans I often say that it is like Christmas, New Year's Day, and the Fourth of July rolled into one. Perhaps I should also suggest that it is as if someone had thrown a giant birthday party, everyone had just gotten a raise and promotion, and the home team had won the big game over the archrival.

For weeks ahead of Tet the Vietnamese begin baking cakes, buying extra supplies of candy and wine, outfitting themselves with new clothes, and decorating their houses with flowers. Relatives come home to worship at family altars, gifts are exchanged, and the colors of red and gold permeate the entire country. It is more important than anything else, even political or ideological differences. And yet one-half hour into the "Year of the Monkey" the Viet Cong launched a major offensive all up and down South Vietnam.

Their attack was a complete surprise, not only because of its timing but also because we had no idea they were in position to launch such a wide-scale operation. They attacked in strength at Dak To, Kontum City, Long Binh, Ben Tre, Saigon, Ban Me Thout, Bien Hoa, Nha Trang, and Hue and at Hoi An, just south of Da Nang. Even here, at one of the largest, most secure bases in South Vietnam, a company of Vietnamese Communists, or Viet Cong, or VC for short, got through to hit the headquarters compound of the Vietnamese I Corps just on the outskirts of Da Nang.

For a week the muzzle blasts of our big guns flashed like summer lightning in the night sky while the artillery rumbled in a continuous roll of thunder. Long strings of glowing tracer rounds spewed down from the orbiting gunships. As I watched each night, I couldn't help but think how strangely beautiful all this was—even though it was caused by human beings trying their level best to kill other human beings.

When I reached my office on the morning of February 8 everyone was frantically trying to keep up with all the changes taking place on the battlefields. The operations officer was talking on two phones simultaneously, the intelligence officer was feverishly trying to evaluate all the incoming reports of enemy attacks, and his NCO was doing his best to keep the big situation map posted. A quick glance at the grease-pencil symbols showing the dispositions of all combat units told me that the VC, despite the surprise and ferocity of their attacks, had been beaten back from just about every objective in the I Corps area. They still occupied Hue, however, and they were also in considerable strength around Quang Tri City.

As I stood there studying the map, Sergeant Howard Duffy came into the office and laid his clipboard on the corner of my desk. Duffy was a clean-cut young man from Nebraska, inordinately proud of the University of Nebraska football team. He was a career NCO on his second tour in Vietnam.

"Ahem," he said, running his hand across his close-cropped blond hair. He had a special way of clearing his throat when he was irritated by something, especially if it was something he thought I could straighten out.

"Okay, Sergeant Duffy, what is it?" I asked without turning around.

"Well, uh, I don't want to bother you none, sir. I mean, if you're busy."

"Oh, I'm sure you don't," I teased. I walked away from the map and sat down, then leaned back in my swivel chair, propped my feet up on the desk, and laced my hands behind my head. "All right, Sergeant, you do recognize this as my 'listening pose,' don't you?"

"Yes, sir."

"So what is it?"

"Colonel Purcell, we're having commo problems at LZ Jane."

"LZ Jane? That's just outside Quang Tri City," I said. I looked back at the map. "Charley is still hanging on in strength around Quang Tri. It's not good to have communications problems at LZ Jane."

"No, sir," Duffy agreed.

"What sort of problems are they having?"

"Radios, sir. The 101st Airborne Division has put a new battalion in there, but they don't have a radio available that'll net with our logistics channel. We need to get a single side band radio up there ASAP. But the thing is, if we send one out, we got no way of knowin' if it'll wind up in the right place. They got 'em a power struggle goin' on between the field and sub-area command. And there's ARVN too. I can't get nowhere by myself, but I figure that you bein' the XO of the 80th and the deputy dog of Da Nang Sub-Area Command, well, sir, maybe you can take care of it."

"Yes, I hear what you're saying, Sergeant. But I was talking to the brigade commander, and Colonel Jones doesn't want us to go directly to one of his subordinate units. We're going to have to work through his communications officer and hope that takes care of it."

"Yes, sir," Sergeant Duffy replied. "Well, if it actually gets as far as the commo officer it'll prob'ly be okay. The thing is, it doesn't always get to him even when that's where it's supposed to go."

I drummed my fingers on the desk for a moment thinking about the problem. Sergeant Duffy had good cause to be frustrated. One of the by-products of fighting a war with so many different lines of command and responsibility was that supplies desperately needed by one element often languished in the supply bins of another. Jealousy and overzealous junior commanders prevented the voluntary distribution of such items. But Duffy was also right when he suggested that I could do something about it. By wearing two hats, executive officer of the 80th General Support Group and deputy commander of the Da Nang Sub-Area Command, I had a foot squarely in each line of command. This was just the type of thing I was supposed to prevent and it was great to have a capable NCO to help me do it.

"All right, Duffy, get me the radio and lay on a helicopter," I ordered. "I will personally hand-carry the radio to the brigade commo officer on my way to check on our unit at Dong Ha. Get word to Captain Drake and have that august young gentleman meet me at the Quang Tri chopper pad at 1400 hours, and I will lay the radio right into his hands."

"Yes, *sir*! Now you're talkin'," Duffy said.

"I just hope he didn't play football for Nebraska," I teased. "If he did, he'll probably fumble as soon as I hand it to him."

"Nevah hoppen, GI," Sergeant Duffy retorted, smiling broadly. "But beggin' your pardon, Colonel, I figure if you'll go up there an' kick a little ass, we'll get some of this crap straightened out."

"Jim Dandy to the rescue. . . ," I sang from a song that we had been hearing on Armed Forces Radio Network.

As my driver drove me out to the airfield, two F-4 Phantom Jets took off, kicking in the afterburners just after they "rotated," or left the ground. They pointed the noses of their fighters nearly straight up and rocketed high into the sky atop two pillars of fire. The roar of their engines spilled out behind them and then rolled across the ground like a tidal wave smashing against everything and everyone in ear-shattering, stomach-shaking majesty. Bombs, rockets, and napalm hung in clusters from the wings, and I knew that within a few minutes they would be dealing out death and destruction to those upstart little pajama-clad people who were challenging the United States. I felt smug, invincible, and proud to be part of the technology that could fight a war with supersonic jets, air-conditioned offices, grease pencils and acetate maps, computers, helicopters, AFN radio, clean sheets, and barbequed steaks.

Five minutes later I was using some of that technology as my helicopter beat its way toward Quang Tri.

Warrant Officer Joe Rose was flying the UH-1 "Huey" and Warrant Officer Dick Ziegler was his copilot. Though warrant officers have been a part of the American army since the days of George Washington, there had never been very many of them—that is, until now. More than half the helicopter pilots in Vietnam were warrant officers. They are afforded the respect of commissioned officers but their specialty is technical, not command. Like the junior officers of the navy, warrant officers are addressed as "mister." They are also sometimes called "chief" although this term is technically correct only if they are in the rank of W-2 or higher.

Our crew chief was SP/4 Robert Chenoweth, and SP/4 Mike Lenker was the door gunner. While Chenoweth and Lenker sat in the doors watching the world slide by beyond the muzzles of their machine guns, Pfc. James E. George, a refrigeration mechanic from my command, sat on the right side of the helicopter in the jump seat.

I always enjoyed my helicopter rides over Vietnam. There was a serenity about them that one could not experience in faster-moving, higher-flying aircraft. It was very pleasant to drift over the lush canopy of trees, the ruggedly beautiful mountains, the broad shining rivers, and picturesque streams.

During such flights I often found myself envying the aircrews because they got to do this several times every day. They could escape the mosquitoes, dust, smell, and noise of Vietnam for these brief "mini–R & Rs," while the rest of us remained stuck on the ground.

The enemy was particularly well entrenched in the ancient capital city of Hue, and as that besieged city was midway between Da Nang and Quang Tri we passed close by during our flight. There was heavy smoke coming from Hue.

Specialist Lenker handed me a headset so that I could hear Mr. Rose.

"You see that smoke down there, sir?" Mr. Rose asked.

"I see it."

"That's the citadel," he explained. "The VC are still in there. This is the third time I've been by here today. We're hittin' 'em with artillery, tear gas, just about everything but the kitchen sink and they're still hangin' on. Unless you need to get a closer look, sir, I'd just as soon give them a lot of room."

I saw a particularly large explosion, even as Mr. Rose was talking about it.

"That's fine with me, Chief," I said. "Stay well clear, there's no sense in getting hit with one of our own artillery rounds."

"I like your thinkin', Colonel," Mr. Rose answered with a grin.

The sky became overcast as we approached Quang Tri, and fifteen minutes later when we started losing altitude for the landing, I could see lacy tendrils of mist trailing the tips of our blades. The rotors were giving the familiar pop-pop-pop sound as we descended through our own rotor wash and I stared through the door at the terrain below: to the west, high, rugged mountains, their tops lost in the low clouds; to the east, sandy beaches and blue ocean. It was actually a very beautiful little place.

As soon as the blades stopped spinning, I saw a Signal Corps officer coming toward the helicopter. It was Captain Drake. Since he was the man I wanted to have the radio, I placed it into his hands. Private George, the refrigeration mechanic, hurried over to repair the disabled reefer truck, which was his mission on this trip. George was an intelligent and ambitious young soldier, and it didn't take him long to find the trouble and make the repair.

Captain Drake and I were standing together on the PSP, the perforated steel planking, which made up the chopper pad. In the hills all around us I could hear the constant thump of artillery and the rattle of small-arms fire. Here and there, wisps of smoke floated up to disappear in the low overcast. "How are things going?" I asked the captain.

"Well, they're out there, sir, all around us," Captain Drake said with a wave of his hand. "But they don't have the strength to overrun our position so it looks like we're in pretty good shape. We can call in artillery, air strikes . . . you name it, we can have it."

"Sounds like if they stay out there much longer they'll be cut to pieces," I said.

"You got it, sir. I hope the bastards stay for a month. By that time we'll have this area bombed so flat we can go out there, pave it over, and turn it into a parking lot."

"Come on now, Captain Drake, you can't win the hearts and minds of these people like that."

The captain smiled broadly. "Yes sir. Well, you might say I have an attitude problem, Colonel, but I don't care about the hearts and minds of these people." He held up the radio. "I do want to thank you for this, though. It was getting to the point that I thought I was going to have to break out the carrier pigeons."

Captain Drake and his commo sergeant got in their jeep and drove off. As I started back toward the helicopter, I saw that the two pilots and Chenoweth had a panel raised and were looking at something.

"What is it?" I asked.

"One of our radios is out," Mr. Rose said, "and I can't climb back up through this overcast without it."

"Do you think there's another one here?"

"No, sir, I wouldn't think so. But it's no big deal, Colonel. We can just fly under the overcast until we get out over the ocean. We'll be okay."

"You're the pilot," I said, climbing back into the aircraft, "but we'll cancel our trip on up to Dong Ha."

When we took off a moment later, Mr. Rose turned the helicopter toward the southeast and headed toward the coast. I noticed that we were flying about three hundred feet or so above the ground—not high enough to be out of range of small-arms fire and certainly not low enough for "nap of the earth" flying, which is to say skimming the surface so as not to provide an easy target for small-arms fire. I started to say something about it, but I didn't.

I should have.

Suddenly I heard an unfamiliar popping sound . . . not like the comforting sound of blades spilling air, but a harsh hammering sound. Warrant Officer Ziegler turned toward me and shouted, "We're being fired on!" His next message was, "We're on fire!"

I looked out the open door and saw the muzzle flashes of three automatic weapons and a line of tracer rounds from each weapon . . . the same tracer rounds I had thought of as beautiful the night before when they were lighting up the sky. But these were not from some orbiting gunship against an unseen enemy on the ground; these were aimed directly at us! They flashed up from the ground and laced into the side of our ship.

For some reason I suddenly thought of Korea and the times those other two officers had volunteered to take my place. I gritted my teeth and waited for the bullet I was certain would slam into my body at any second. It seemed that I was about to be "called out" on strike three.

The helicopter gave a sudden lurch and then the inside flared brightly with an orange light. Fire on board an aircraft is something you can read about or talk about philosophically, but in order to really understand how quickly it gets hot enough to melt metal, you have to experience it. Only seconds after the first round hit, the fire was already that hot just forward of the transmission housing in the center of the passenger compartment of our helicopter. Private George and I were fortunate to be sitting on the outside seats as far away from the heat as it was possible to be.

"We're going down!" Mr. Ziegler shouted.

The helicopter made a sweeping turn to the right and hurtled toward the ground trailing fire and smoke. Mr. Rose fought to control the helicopter and to land it as quickly as possible. We were headed down toward the only open area in sight—a sandy cemetery. There was nothing the rest of us could do but hang on . . . and pray.

I prayed. I have never prayed with more intensity or sincerity than at that moment. I prayed with every ounce of my being.

The helicopter hit hard, so hard that the tips of the rotor blades dug into the ground and then broke as they struck a large granite monument. There was no explosion, but the helicopter was ripped to shreds by the ground impact and the flailing rotor blades. I felt the seat belt dig into me as I was thrown forward.

I've never heard such a noise or felt such a jarring impact. My teeth banged together so hard that my gums hurt, and something, or someone, slammed against my side. "Get out! Everybody out!" the pilot shouted as soon as we quit bouncing around.

The engine noise was gone now but there was still a roaring sound in my ears. For a moment I didn't know what the roaring was. Then I realized it was fire. We were sitting on hundreds of gallons of flaming jet fuel.

I thought of all the television shows I had seen where an airplane erupted into a gigantic ball of fire. I knew that was about to happen to us and we had to get away quickly.

George, Chenoweth, Lenker, and I loosened our seat belts and jumped out, but the pilot and copilot couldn't get out through their respective doors. They were trapped in their seats by the "chicken plates," as the aircrews humorously called the armor shields installed between them and their doors. The door gunner ran to the front doors and slid the panels back so Mr. Rose and Mr. Ziegler could get out. By the time he opened their doors, though, the pilots had already butted their way through the windshield, and they fell on the sand in front of our burning chopper.

"Hey, I'm hit . . . I'm hit in the leg!" Mr. Ziegler said in surprise as he stood up to shake off the sand. I don't think he realized he had been hit until that moment.

"My weapon!" Private George called.

"Leave it!" I shouted, but not hearing me, he ran back to the ship to recover his M-14 rifle, which was lying on the floor between the pilots' seats.

I don't know what George was thinking at the time . . . whether he thought he could move so quickly that the fire couldn't get him or whether he was actually more concerned with what he believed to be his duty than he was with his personal safety. Whatever it was that motivated him, it drove him right into the middle of the flames.

The fire engulfed him instantly and Specialist Lenker and I had to reach in and drag him out. Even then it was already too late. His clothes were burning and smoke was coming from beneath his helmet. George began rolling on the ground and Lenker helped him put out the flames by smothering them with his own flak jacket. Flames had licked at George's hands and face, and his skin there was hanging in strips. But he had succeeded in recovering his rifle.

We could hear enemy soldiers shouting in the distance, getting closer by the second. It was very difficult to determine which direction the enemy were approaching from, but we had to make a move very quickly.

"Colonel, we had better get away from this thing," Mr. Rose said.

"You're right. Let's go," I answered. Because Lenker and I still had hold of George, we half-carried and half-dragged the badly burned young soldier as we moved away from the burning helicopter. Mr. Ziegler was limping badly but was able to move a safe distance away from the chopper. As Lenker and I tended to George, Rose and Chenoweth helped Mr. Ziegler bandage his wound.

There was no explosion. At least not the big, booming kind you see in the movies. The flames just got bigger and bigger until the fuselage was a roaring inferno. When I looked back it was hard to believe that we had all been sitting inside that thing just seconds before. If we had been another hundred feet higher, we surely would not have made it down to the ground in one piece.

Suddenly there was a series of popping sounds like very loud popcorn or rifle fire. At first we were all startled but then realized it was just the ammunition that remained in the door guns' chute "cooking off."

I asked Mr. Ziegler if he had gotten a mayday call off.

"No, sir, there wasn't enough time."

That was almost as bitter a blow as getting shot down. If he had been able to get out a mayday call, we might have expected a relief patrol of friendlies at any moment. But without the call we could only hope that someone friendly saw us. The overcast, our position outside of Quang Tri, and the altitude we were flying when we were hit made that seem unlikely. It was immediately clear to me that we were going to have to face the situation with whatever means we had with us, because we could not count any help.

I looked around at our surroundings. The cemetery's grave markers stood in silent protest at our violent intrusion of this peaceful glade. At that, we were fortunate to have been near open ground. If we had been over the jungle not one of us would have survived the fiery crash.

Our helicopter was obviously not the only thing to disturb the peace of the dead, for just ahead of us was a large crater carved out of the earth by a bomb or an artillery shell. I pointed toward it.

"Let's get in there," I ordered.

Moving as quickly as we could under the circumstances, we made for the hole, then slid down into it and looked back toward the helicopter. With the roaring orange flames and the towering pillar of black, oily smoke, we couldn't have been more clearly marked if there had been a big neon sign with an arrow pointing right at us.

I pulled out my .38 revolver and examined it closely. There were only five rounds loaded in the cylinder. As a safety precaution in the event the pistol was accidentally dropped I always left the chamber under the hammer empty. I had fired this pistol on the range only last week, even though my staff had offered to "pencil qualify" me, for I had always found a trip to the range very relaxing. But this wasn't the range and I wouldn't be shooting at man-sized silhouettes; I would be shooting at living human beings. For the first time ever the pistol felt strange, foreign to me. Suddenly I realized that I had better take stock of our defensive capability.

"What are our weapons?" I asked, looking around.

"Mike and I have pistols," Mr. Ziegler said.

"I brought my door gun," Chenoweth said, "but it has a broken sear." This meant that once he pulled the trigger, the gun would continue to fire until it was out of ammunition or until it jammed. There was only a short belt of ammunition with the gun, and it was already full of sand. I was not sure that the gun would even fire. Private George had gone back for his rifle but he was in no position to use it. Rose held it now. But he was a W-1, a warrant officer not too long out of flight school, and I wondered if he had ever qualified with this particular weapon.

"We have three pistols, one rifle, and the door gun," I said, counting aloud.

"What are we going to do, Colonel?" Mr. Rose asked.

I looked at Mr. Ziegler and Private George. Ziegler's leg was bleeding, and Private George was in great pain and groaning softly.

"Mr. Ziegler, take George with you and sneak out the back of this crater and head for those trees," I ordered. "If we can draw their attention to us the two of you might be able to make it back to Captain Drake's unit at Quang Tri. The rest of us will keep the VC occupied for as long as possible."

"Let's go, George," Ziegler said.

"You go on," George said. "I don't think I can do it."

"Come on, try," Ziegler urged.

George gritted his teeth and climbed up the back of the hole. Ziegler went up after him.

"Ah, you're looking good," Ziegler said. I knew that Mr. Ziegler was hurting as well and I respected his attempt to help Private George.

The two wounded men moved slowly toward the wooded area while the rest of us stared out in the direction of the burning wreckage. I listened as they crawled away, hearing the scuffling sound they made against the ground and the pained, labored breathing of George. I knew that each breath he took was agony and my heart went out to him. But I also knew that I was responsible for the rest of us—four of us now, armed with only two pistols, one rifle, and a defective machine gun, against an as yet unknown number of enemy armed with who knew what. I knew for a certainty that they were armed with at least three automatic weapons, the ones that had brought us down.

I suspected the VC would first check out the area around the crash site before looking for any passengers. I looked at my pistol again and saw that I had gotten dirt on it. I blew the dirt away, blowing softly because I was afraid the VC would hear me. Then we waited.

3

CAPTURE

BEN'S STORY

I watched as Ziegler and George moved toward the tree line. It seemed to take them forever, and I had the unpleasant thought that creeping across the open ground as they were, they were as exposed as a couple of wounded bugs crawling across a kitchen table. When at last they disappeared from view I looked back around our hole and saw that everyone else had been watching them just as intently.

"We're making too high a profile," I said. "Everybody get down in the bottom of the hole except one person."

"I'll keep a lookout," Rose volunteered.

"All right. Chenoweth, Lenker, you two get down here with me," I ordered.

We got as low into the depression as we could, and I looked into Chenoweth's and Lenker's faces. Both were frightened but neither looked as if he were about to panic. I leaned my head back against the side of the crater and looked up. At that very moment a jet was passing high overhead. The pilot was probably on his way to Saigon, or even Bangkok, totally unaware of the tiny life-and-death struggle we were waging down here.

Was it just this morning that I had contemplated with such satisfaction the wonders of a technological war? Where were those things now? Where were the clean sheets, the air conditioner, the electric typewriter? Right now I would have been satisfied with four well-trained infantry soldiers armed with rifles that I could be sure would work. I smiled at the irony of it, and Chenoweth and Lenker, if they saw me, must have thought I was a little crazy.

"Colonel, someone's coming," Mr. Rose whispered.

"Maybe it's ARVNs or Vietnamese militia," Chenoweth suggested hopefully.

ARVN meant Army of the Republic of Vietnam, the good guys. It could be; they were in Quang Tri, they saw us take off, and they may have seen us get hit. If so, it would be only natural that they would send a patrol to bring us back.

Full of hope I clambered up to the top of the crater and looked out toward the men coming toward us. My heart sank.

The men coming toward us weren't in uniform. If they were the good guys, even the militia, they would have been. And some of the weapons they were carrying were the short, distinctively ugly but very effective AK-47s. Definitely not good-guy weapons.

Mr. Rose recognized it as quickly as I did. "Colonel, they're . . . ," he started, but he couldn't make himself finish the statement.

"VC," I went on for him.

I looked around the hole at the men who were with me and at the determination on their faces. Chenoweth was trying to brush the dirt off the ammo belt for the door gun. Rose chambered a round in George's M-14 and unlocked the safety. Lenker cocked his pistol, and I heard the mechanism slide back and forth as he got ready to fire the weapon. He inched up to the edge of the hole and looked toward the approaching men.

"One, two, three," Lenker started counting softly. A moment later he said in a quiet, frightened voice, "Colonel, I count twelve of them."

"Are you guys any good with those things?" I asked.

"Are you kidding?" Rose replied. "All I can do is make noise with it."

"Colonel, the receiver is full of dirt," Chenoweth said. "I won't get off more'n one or two rounds."

"I've never qualified with a .45," Lenker added unhelpfully.

The VC were close enough now that we could hear them talking back and forth in excited voices. They had just shot down a helicopter, perhaps the single most identifiable symbol of their enemy, and they were all high as kites. They weren't about to be denied a final victory by two pistols, one rifle, and one defective machine gun. I looked at the pistol in my hand and then at the men who were with me. If we opened fire we might get one or two of them, but we would be overrun almost instantly and every one of us would be killed.

I thought of the Code of Conduct.

If I am in command, I will never surrender my men so long as we have the means to resist.

I recalled all the classes I had taught on the code, and I could almost see the shining faces of American kids sitting in the bleachers in the training areas at places like Fort Leonard Wood, Fort Bragg, and Fort Benning, anxious for the class to be over so they could go back for lunch. But we weren't in a training area, and there was no bus waiting behind the bleachers to take the troops to the mess hall. We were in Vietnam, lying in a bomb crater, while our helicopter burned a few hundred yards away. And we were surrounded by Viet Cong soldiers, all carrying assorted automatic rifles: AK-47s and captured American BARs and M-16s. I looked around to make sure that Ziegler and George were still out of sight.

"Anybody see Ziegler and George?" I asked.

"I think they're well back in the trees now, Colonel," Chenoweth said.

My two wounded were out of sight. There was nothing more I could do for them right now. I closed my eyes for a moment. . . . *So long as we have the means to resist,* the Code of Conduct says. Do we have the means to resist? Or do we have only the means to trade our four lives for one or two of theirs? Almost instantly afterward a concussion grenade exploded five meters in front of our crater. The next one could explode inside the crater.

I took a deep breath and then made the most difficult decision I was ever called upon to make.

"Men, we do not have the necessary weapons to fight them," I said with a tight voice. "It would be suicide to start a fire fight."

Chenoweth stood up and raised his hands over his head. The first VC who saw him shouted something to the others, and they all ran over to our crater pointing their rifles toward us. They were excited, shouting, and laughing, celebrating the fact that they had not only shot down a helicopter but captured the Americans who were flying it.

I didn't realize I was still holding the pistol until they were right on me. Then one of the group—I assumed he was the leader because he was wearing an armband—waved his weapon at me.

"Hands up!" he shouted. "Hands up!"

When I lifted my hands I felt a sharp pain in my right side, and I realized then that I must have broken some ribs during the crash. The VC searched us not very gently but very thoroughly.

"Where are others?"

"There aren't any others," I answered. "Just the four of us."

Armband pointed to the burning helicopter. "We know that carries ten," he said. "Where are others?"

"You don't carry ten every time you go up," Rose said. "This is all of us."

A few of the VC had already begun to look in the woods around the cemetery and one of them let out a shout. Several others ran toward him. They had found George.

Armband smiled. "You see," he said. "I know you lie." Apparently Ziegler was still evading.

I heard George give a cry of pain and I looked toward him. "Be careful," I said. "He's wounded."

The VC nearest Armband hit me between the shoulder blades with the butt of his rifle. I felt pain stab all through me and I had to take a stutter step to keep from falling.

"You do not worry about him," Armband said.

"I *will* worry about him," I replied. "He's one of my men."

"You be quiet. I am in command," Armband said. He pointed to my pockets. "You give."

"What do you want?"

One of them reached for my pockets. "You give," Armband said again, more insistently this time.

We emptied our pockets for them and they took every personal possession we had: billfolds with identification cards, driver's licenses, and pictures of our families. Then they took my college ring and the wristwatch Anne had given me just before I left Boonville. When they reached for my wedding band, I pulled my hand back.

"No," I said. "This reminds me of my wife. It's not worth anything to you . . . it's very important to me."

"You give!"

"No."

One of the VC pulled out a large knife.

"Give it to 'em, Colonel. Else they'll cut your finger off and take it anyway," Specialist Lenker said.

Reluctantly I pulled the ring off my finger. It had been so long since I had taken the ring off that for a moment I was afraid it wasn't going to come off. Then I felt a momentary panic because I was afraid they really would cut my finger off. Finally the ring slipped off, and it's no exaggeration to say that I felt a stabbing pain in my heart.

"Take off boots," Armband ordered.

"No, I'm not going to take off my boots. What do you want our boots for?" Mr. Rose asked.

"You will not need boots," Armband said angrily, and several of his men looked ready to shoot us.

We sat down and took off our boots. For some strange reason I recalled vividly putting them on that morning. I could remember sitting on the edge of my bed, looking down at the black toe and green nylon of the jungle boots and thinking what ugly footgear we were wearing in this war. That was no more than eight hours before. What a drastic and unexpected change had occurred in my life in a few short hours! One minute I was a productive officer straightening out a logistics problem, and the next minute I was in a struggle for my life. It all happened so quickly that there was no time to adjust.

The VC took the shoelaces from the boots and used them to tie our thumbs together behind our backs. Then they tied our arms together with a rope above the elbows.

"Move," Armband said, poking me in the ribs with the muzzle of his AK-47. He must've hit one of the broken ribs because there was a sudden, excruciating stab of pain, and I gasped aloud from it. Slowly we started to walk toward the small hamlet nearby. As soon as we entered the hamlet we were ordered to "face the wall." This command alarmed us all, for only a few days before we had read about five marines who had been found shot to death with their hands tied behind their backs. With as much conviction as I could muster, I told the others that we were more valuable to the VC alive than dead. As it turned out, the VC only wanted to keep us from seeing the Vietnamese living in the hamlet while we paused there for a few minutes.

We started walking again. We walked more quickly now across a muddy rice paddy to a nearby canal, where we were loaded onto two sampans. I was placed in one sampan with George, while Rose, Chenoweth, and Lenker were directed to get into the other. There was a very unsettling quietness all around us; nothing was moving. Then George asked, "Colonel, are you a Christian?"

"Yes, son, I am."

"Could you maybe say a prayer with me?"

"I would very much like to pray with you," I answered.

There on that boat, with the smell of fish, jungle, and charcoal braziers filling our nostrils, that terribly burned young soldier and I prayed. We asked for courage and strength to face the unknown future. Prayer has always meant a lot to me, but at that particular moment it became the glue that was holding the broken pieces of my life together.

After a brief trip down the canal we got out of the sampans near another hamlet and were paraded down the street for the inhabitants to see. We walked on through the hamlet and then along a small narrow path that led toward the mountains in the distance. We walked all night long and by the next morning our feet were raw with cuts, bruises, and broken blisters.

George was still suffering terribly and I honestly don't

know how he had lasted this long. By now he could no longer
see to walk because his badly burned face had swollen to the
degree that his eyes were shut. By the time we reached the
mountains George had reached his limit. But other than a few
quiet, almost apologetic moans of pain, he said nothing. He
tried to stay with us, but he began stumbling around, falling
every two or three steps.

"You go!" Armband said to him. "You make everyone
slow!"

George tried to get up but he fell again.

"You go!"

"Can't you see how badly wounded he is?" I asked.
"You must get medical attention for this man immediately."

"Quiet! You be quiet!" one of the VC replied. He
pointed his AK-47 at me.

I was tired, dispirited, in pain, and still shamed over having surrendered. If he was going to shoot, let him shoot. I
stared at Armband.

"I want a doctor for this man," I said again.

"You be quiet. You not in charge. I am in charge," Armband said. "If you speak again I will have you shot."

This was it, the first real challenge since we were captured. It was a good time to meet the challenge, too. I was
about at my limits.

"If you're going to shoot, do it!" I challenged. "But I
want a doctor for this man. *Bac si,* do you understand? *Bac
si, bac si,*" I said, using the Vietnamese word for doctor.

For a long moment it was a contest of will between the
VC who was holding the rifle and me. Finally Armband gave
a small nod to the guard and the VC lowered his gun. I realized then that I wasn't about to be killed . . . at least not
now.

"Yes, yes, *bac si,*" he answered. He said something in
Vietnamese, and two VC moved George to the side of the
trail and sat him down, rather gently I thought, in comparison
with the way we had been treated since our capture. I felt
a sense of relief. At least one of my men would find some
peace.

I walked over to Private George and looked down at
him. I wanted to put my hand on his shoulder, to comfort

him in some way, but my hands were still tied behind my back. George wasn't that much older than my son David, and I wished with all my heart I could do something to ease his suffering.

"James," I said. "Or do they call you Jimmy?"

"Some call me James, some call me Jimmy," he answered in a quiet, frightened voice.

"James, you're going to stay here until a doctor comes."

"Colonel, would you . . . would you say the Lord's Prayer with me?"

I got on my knees beside him and we started to pray.

"No!" Armband shouted at me. "No, you can not do that! You go! You go now!"

I didn't move. Together James George and I repeated the Lord's Prayer, and never in the most magnificent cathedral or the smallest chapel have the words meant more to me than they did then.

"You go!" Armband said again. I heard the metallic sound of a bolt being slammed home and I knew that Armband had cocked his weapon. I felt the barrel on the back of my neck, but I didn't move. I continued to say the Lord's Prayer aloud with James.

Armband let out a bellow of rage and turned away, jerking the gun away with him. I wondered why he was so angry, why he was so against allowing George this comfort. Then, with an insight that was born of that travail, I realized what it was. He was frightened. He was frightened at coming face to face with a faith that was stronger than fear.

"Thank you, Colonel," George said when the prayer was finished. "I'll be all right now. Whatever happens, it'll be all right."

"Okay! Go! You go now!" Armband shouted, lifting me back to my feet and shoving me with the barrel of the gun. I joined the others and we were herded up the trail. I looked around once and saw one of the VC standing behind George. The VC guard nearest me clubbed me right between the shoulders, forcing me to look back to the front. After we had moved out of sight of George, we heard a shot. Startled, I looked around, but I could no longer see George.

"What was that?" I asked. "What was that shot?"

"Someone shoot, it means nothing," Armband said.

"I want to go back."

"No."

"Did you shoot Private George?"

Armband looked at me for a moment; then he shook his head.

"No," he said. "We get *bac si* for your GI."

I must confess that in my exhaustion I let myself believe him because I wanted to believe him. And in the war zone one did hear random shots all the time, so a single gunshot wasn't in itself significant. But down inside, I wondered, Did they shoot George? I didn't know. I honestly didn't know. Maybe I did. But I wanted to believe. Please, God, I wanted to believe.

I felt so alone.

4

MISSING IN ACTION

ANNE'S STORY

This was the last letter I wrote to Ben before I learned he had been shot down and was missing in action. At the time I wrote it he was already a prisoner of the Viet Cong, although I had no way of knowing that. I was still making happy plans for seeing him in Hawaii while Ben, with his arms tied behind his back and his feet raw and bleeding, was being pushed through the jungle at the point of a gun.

Boonville, Missouri
February 9, 1968

Dear Ben,
I'm very excited over the R & R plans. I went to Columbia today and talked with the travel agent about my trip. I can fly out of St. Louis at 10:00 A.M., change planes in Los Angeles, and arrive in Hawaii at 7:15 P.M., Hawaiian time. That's a good schedule for me, so all you need to decide now is the exact date in March that we can meet for R & R. Check your schedule and let me know when you can meet me, and I'll take care of the details here.

We are all well. The children are busy in school and, of course, the snow keeps us busy shoveling and trying to get the car started in the morning. For that one reason alone I would be glad for a tour of duty in the South.

Dr. Avery seems to think Cliff's stomachaches are stress related. Ben, Cliff has made the statement, "I'm afraid Daddy won't come home." We are just not going to watch the TV newscasts anymore. The news is broadcast from the battlefields in Vietnam and brings the war right into our living room. It has been reported that some families have actually seen their sons and husbands wounded as they watch the telecasts. I'm sure this is enough to make Cliff uneasy. After all, he's only seven. You know, when your children hurt, it's a hurt that can cut deeply into a parent's heart.

Yesterday, I was attending an all-day associational Woman's Missionary Union meeting at a small church just south of Boonville. I couldn't put my finger on what was causing it, but I suddenly began experiencing a terrible sense of foreboding, an apprehension about your safety. During our lunchtime I found a quiet place by myself and I prayed for us.

Are you all right? Are you safe and well? I certainly hope everything is going okay. I miss you so very much, and every day I see how important it is for families to have both mom and dad around. I know soldiers and their families must be the people most devoted to peace since they feel the effects of war most directly.

On our countdown calendar we have almost reached the halfway mark. Since you left in August, we have marked off 161 days. The calendar hangs right beside our kitchen table and we mark off one more day while we are having our evening meal. It helps us realize that your return is getting closer and closer, one day at a time.

Next time we communicate I'll send a tape so that all the children can share with you. I was just too tired tonight to get everything ready to make a tape.

Good night. I love you and I'm not mad at you.

ANNE

Being involved with the church during Ben's absence was very good for me—not only for the great spiritual comfort I received from the worship, but also because it kept me busy during the time Ben would be away. On Monday night, the twelfth of February, there had been a community-wide church service at the First Baptist Church in Boonville. Every Baptist church in the area, black and white, had participated in the service. For me it was a particularly uplifting experience, and I was already thinking of things I could tell Ben about it in my next letter . . . or better yet, share with him on the R & R.

With half of Ben's tour completed and the prospect of spending an R & R in Hawaii with him but a few days away, all was right with my world. When the service was over I walked down the hall to the back of our Sunday School Annex to get Joy and Sherri from the nursery. Debbie had attended the service with me and was still out front visiting with some friends. Cliff and David were home doing homework. As I walked by our pastor's study I saw Reverend Clemons standing in the doorway of his office. With him were Major Jim Statler and Major Statler's wife, Bonnie. When Ben volunteered for duty in Vietnam, Jim had replaced him as professor of military science at Kemper Military School in Boonville.

A chill passed over me, as surely as if the cold, outside wind had suddenly found its way into the friendly warmth of this church hall. I stopped in my tracks, for I knew that Jim was there to tell me something about Ben, that he was wounded . . . or worse, that he was dead.

"Anne, would you please come into my study?" Reverend Clemons asked, and although he tried to keep his voice as normal as possible, I could hear his concern even before I knew the problem.

Cold and numb, I followed them into his study. Reverend Clemons asked me to sit down. He may have even helped me; I honestly don't know. My heart was in my mouth, and the dread and fear I felt were something palpable.

"It's . . . it's Ben, isn't it?" I asked quietly. "Please, God, he isn't dead?"

"No, he isn't dead," Jim said quickly. "At least, they don't think he is."

Jim's answer made no sense to me.

"They don't think he's dead? What do you mean they don't think he's dead?"

"He was on a helicopter that was shot down on the eighth of February," Jim said. "He's missing in action."

"The eighth? That's four days ago."

"The helicopter wasn't spotted until the next day," Jim explained. "A search party was sent out to look around the area. The search party was attacked by VC and one of the party was wounded. I'm sure that's the reason for the delay in notification. Anyway, they didn't find any bodies . . . so they are reasonably certain everyone survived the crash."

"Missing," I said, trying to make the word register.

I sat there for a long moment not saying another thing. I'm sure Reverend Clemons, as well as Jim and Bonnie, were saying comforting things to me and I was gratified for their concern, but I didn't hear another word that was said.

I can remember once, when I was a little girl, I fell from a tree and had the breath knocked from my body. I lay there on the ground for a long moment then, frightened by what had happened to me, wondering why I couldn't breathe or even if I would ever breathe again. I felt just like that now.

Before Ben had left for Vietnam we had talked one evening about the possibility of his being killed. It was like buying life insurance. It's not something you want to face, and yet you know the possibility is there so you face it. We talked about what the children and I would do if Ben were killed. But we had never discussed MIA and POW status or even dreamed that something like that might happen. Now I wished we had.

I'm not proud of the first thought that raced through my mind. It was very self-pitying and very selfish. I thought, "Oh! If I just didn't have the children!"

I felt alone and incapable of caring for myself, much less assuming the total responsibility for five children with—and I had to be honest with myself—little real hope of Ben's ever returning. I was in a most undesirable situation but it was very real. I couldn't back out no matter how badly I might want to escape.

"Let's hold hands and pray," Reverend Clemons suggested.

I took his hand and Bonnie's, and we made a circle there in his study while he prayed. He prayed for Ben, for his care and safety, and for the children and myself. I don't remember crying. I don't think I did. I was just too shocked. And though I couldn't remember exactly what was said to me in the way of comfort, I do remember a warm hug that Bonnie Statler gave me. There was a feeling of love, understanding, and caring in that hug.

Reverend Clemons and the Statlers followed me and the girls home. I had not yet told Debbie what had happened, and when she noticed the cars following us she was excited because she thought we were going to have an after-church get-together with friends.

When we got home I called David and Cliff from their studies and asked them to come into the living room. As they came in, David read something in my face, and I saw an instant expression of concern register on his. I started to speak, but I found I couldn't say the words, so Reverend Clemons spoke for me.

"Children, I'm afraid I have some sad news to tell you," he said. "Your father has been reported missing in action."

For a moment the children stood there, as shocked at receiving this terrible news as I had been . . . and as unable to accept it. Again Reverend Clemons asked us to hold hands and again we made a circle, larger this time, as he prayed for Ben and for us.

Suddenly Debbie ran from the living room into her bedroom, where she flung herself on her bed and cried. I thought her heart would break, and watching her experience such an acute pain nearly broke mine. Being in a state of shock and pain myself, I could not give my daughter any comfort. I felt helpless . . . devastated.

When I received word of Ben's crash I was told also that Ben's mother would be given word the next morning by a military officer from North Georgia College in Dahlonega, Georgia. I didn't want Mom to be alone when she got that awful news, so I phoned Reverend Furman Lewis, who was pastor of Bethlehem Baptist Church in Clarkesville and who also happened to live next door to Mom. I told him about the MIA report and asked him if he would be present with Ben's mother when she heard the news. He agreed immediately and was there the next morning when the officer arrived. Through the terrible years that followed, Reverend Lewis and his wife, Jeanette, were there for Mom when she needed them. During that time, also, members of Bethlehem Church prayed for Ben and all the POWs and MIAs, believing their prayers would be answered.

I held on and played the role of the strong army wife and the dutiful mother for as long as I could that night. Finally the anguish became too much and I could no longer keep the tears back. I cried. I cried as if there were no end to my tears. My life lay crumbled at my feet, and I had no desire to attempt to put it back together, especially if putting it back together meant I would have to live a life without Ben.

My sorrow and anguish were also crowded with self-pity. All I could see were five children and too much responsibility for a woman to handle alone. And there were the house and the car. What would I do about the car? Ben had always taken care of things like tires and oil and batteries and such. I'd always been intimidated by the slightest mechanical problem. Even with Ben in Vietnam, he would occasionally remind me to change the oil, check the antifreeze, get a tune-up, and so on, and of course I could write him letters and ask him about things. What would I do now?

Questions ran through my mind, not in any orderly procession, but tumbling over each other in a flood of confusion: Where will we go to live? What will I do about this house? How will I take care of the kids? How can I live without Ben and without any hope for his return?

Just thinking all this scared me so much that I wanted to run away and hide. When I thought of the horrors Ben must be going through, I wasn't sure that I even wanted to live.

Somewhere in the back of my mind, a little candle flame flickered. This tiny flame was the vestige of my faith. It was telling me where I could turn for help, but despite a lifetime of church activity I have to admit that in that moment of crisis my faith was very, very weak. The glow of that candle didn't go out that night, but neither did it flare up into a comforting light.

Missing in action, I knew, could mean many things. There had been a helicopter crash. How could Ben have gone through that without suffering some grievous injury? Was he wounded? If so, how badly? Was he dying from the wounds? Had he already died, and I just didn't know it?

He had been missing since the eighth of February, and yet in the four days since then I had continued to live my life just as if he were safe and secure in his quarters, in his office, or at the Chapel of Flags. Would I *ever* know anything definite about what had happened on that day? Would I ever see him again or know his fate? I needed a solid rock to put my dangling feet upon—a starting point from which to put my world together again.

The next day I told the children that they didn't have to go to school if they didn't want to. They chose to go—perhaps to hang onto something familiar and safe.

Something happened to David that I found poignant. During PE class the teacher asked him about his dad. David didn't have the heart to tell him the latest news. He just said, "Dad's fine." He was afraid he would cry in front of his friends if he told the truth, and to a fourteen-year-old boy that would have been horribly embarrassing.

Debbie, ten, and Cliff, eight, also kept the news to themselves. I learned later that Cliff had found a large tree on the outer edge of the playground and for several days sat there alone during recess. Sherri, five, and Joy, two, were too young to understand fully the terrible sadness that the rest of us were carrying.

I realized that Ben probably hadn't even received my letter about R & R. Just thinking about those plans now made me sad. I realized, also, that our communication would be stopped—the monthly phone call, the letters and tapes. Oh, how terribly I was going to miss keeping in touch.

How alone I felt. How easily the tears flowed, and how very much my reactions affected the children. I tried to be strong but it was hard . . . oh, it was hard.

MIA wife. What a horrible category! It's like being in limbo—maybe a wife, maybe a widow; nothing definite to put my mind at rest. I didn't know where to turn or what would happen next. I was very afraid.

Our friends in Boonville were very supportive, and I was grateful for each one of them. Also, we had a great church and a caring church family. Mary and John Ball, for example, kept close contact and brought food. Mary came to play with Sherri, who was five years old and didn't understand what was making her world so sad.

The news I had received had shaken my faith, and I wasn't able to ask God for anything except, "Help me, dear Father." God answered my prayers, though, without demanding that they be specific. I hung onto this important truth, and the flickering flame of my candle of faith began to grow just a little brighter.

Five days after I first heard the news of Ben's status I led our church's Woman's Missionary Union in a social program at the Boonville Training Center for Boys. We had been planning this program for several months, but now just the thought of having to share my feelings with anyone made me cry out in protest. Yet I knew this was an important program. Others were counting on me as the president of WMU.

Reverend Clemons came by for me on Saturday, and reluctantly I accompanied him to the training center. I was able to get through the program, and I even managed to smile a little, although I was dying on the inside.

When I returned home I saw something that I will always regard as a sign of comfort and hope. As I walked up the sidewalk toward the front porch I saw a snow-white dove sitting in our yard. While doves were fairly common in our neighborhood, white doves were not. I thought this one was particularly beautiful, and it sat very still and very quiet. Even when I walked close by it didn't fly away.

Later when I thought about that dove, I felt that God must have sent it to remind me that he is always near. I derived a great deal of comfort from that thought, for I knew that no matter how dark the day may seem, God is always the bright spot I can count on. I hope I will always remember this.

I also received a great deal of comfort from our Sunday school lessons during the weeks immediately following Ben's disappearance. We were studying the Book of James, and I particularly liked a passage from James 1:2–5.

> Is your life full of difficulties and temptations? Then be happy, for when the way is rough, your patience has a chance to grow. So let it grow, and don't try to squirm out of your problems. For when your patience is finally in full bloom, then you will be ready for anything, strong in character, full and complete. If you want to know what God wants you to do, ask Him and He will gladly tell you.

This version was from the *Living Bible* and I felt that the colloquial words spoke to me as surely as if they had been written just for me. The wonderful thing about it was that although the Sunday school lessons are prepared months before they are printed and distributed, God saw to it that these meaningful words were available for me just when I needed them most.

Although my faith was beginning to grow stronger, I was still struggling to be the happy, productive mother I needed to be for the sake of my children. They were hurting terribly but were too young to know how to share their feelings. And to be honest, I was afraid I was so wrapped up in my own world of frustration that I didn't see, or recognize, their needs.

I found it extremely difficult to go to places Ben and I had visited together because the memories came flooding back, and I found myself not even wanting to leave the house. I knew I couldn't live that way, so I forced myself to do things and to go places. Once I did make the effort, I found the next time wasn't quite as painful. Bern and Jaci Draper invited me to a concert in Columbia, Missouri. Reluctantly I made myself go with them. I realized that having special friends to share time with made going out a little more bearable. It would have been so easy to sit down and let the world go by, but I couldn't do that. I had spent my entire life believing that a person's burdens can be eased by letting Christ into their lives. Now I wanted to demonstrate that faith, especially to my children. I wanted to do that, but I had a long way to go to make it happen.

5

FIRST CAMP

BEN'S STORY

It had been five days since the helicopter had crashed in flames and burned in the cemetery, and I wondered if Anne knew about it yet. What had she been told? Did she know I was still alive? Were the children aware of my situation? I knew she and the children would be anxious about my welfare, and I wanted to get in touch with them as soon as I could to put their minds at rest.

Of the six Americans who were on board that helicopter when it took off from Quang Tri, there were only four still together: Joe Rose, the pilot; Robert Chenoweth, the crew chief; Michael Lenker, the door gunner; and me. We still hadn't seen Dick Ziegler, the copilot who had managed to slip away just before the group was captured.

Of James George we knew nothing. Our last view of him was as he sat alongside the trail, an armed VC behind him, waiting, Armband had assured us, for a doctor. I could only hope and pray that he was safe. I feared for his welfare.

After we were captured we began walking in a westerly direction into the mountains south and west of Khe Sanh. We could hear the battle raging. The burst of bombs and artillery shells split the jungle air with a deafening roar. Despite the nearness of the battle, however, we felt far, far away.

On the second day my hands were untied. My thumbs had been tied together for twenty-four consecutive hours, and even after the strings were removed, my thumbs were so numb that I could barely feel them.

Every step I took was excruciating. My feet became a solid mass of blisters. I crawled up the mountain trails, mostly on hands and knees, and slid down the rain-slickened paths on the other side on my rear end, heels, and hands. The pain in my right side didn't make the walking any easier. Although there was no way to tell for sure, I strongly suspected that at least two and possibly three ribs had been cracked during the crash of our helicopter.

As if blistered feet and broken ribs weren't trouble enough, we were constantly plagued by thirst and hunger. We had had nothing to eat so far but two handfuls of boiled rice and a total of two cups of water to drink. The days had been overcast, and a slight drizzle fell on us for most of our journey. This concealed our movement from friendly aircraft, but at least it had one beneficial effect. As moisture accumulated on the leaves, droplets of water formed on the bottom tips. From time to time I would pause long enough to put my tongue under a leaf and catch a drop of water. The guard wasn't all that understanding, however, for he'd immediately chamber a round in his AK-47 and start screaming, *"Dee, dee. Dee, dee."* That meant "go."

There were times on the trail during those first few days that I wanted to give up. But at my moments of greatest despair I would think of Anne, I would see her face, and I would feel her love. It was a great comfort to know that someone cared and was waiting for me. It was the assurance of that love that made me want to go on.

We walked throughout the first night but were allowed to stop and rest on the next four. We didn't rest very well. The roofs over our little lean-tos leaked, and there was nothing to protect our wet bodies from the cold night air as we lay on the damp ground. By morning our muscles were stiff and sore and our bones creaked.

Late in the afternoon of the thirteenth we stopped at a

small hut in the mountains several miles west of where we were captured. Here Armband and his men left us, turning us over to a new team of Vietnamese guards and a new headman. The new headman had an unusually long nose so I thought of him as Hooknose. The hut appeared to be new and had a good roof. Thank goodness, I thought, for small favors.

I looked around inside the hut as well as I could before it grew too dark for me to see. Our "host" was a Montagnard, or mountain man, who apparently lived alone in the cabin, which was about ten feet wide and twenty feet long. The man had a small straw bed for himself at one end and a bed made of woven sticks for prisoners at the other. He also had one hen and a bin of rice, which he used to feed prisoners and VC soldiers who might pass his way. I didn't know if he was cooperating with the VC from choice or necessity. He kept to himself over in the corner of the little room and didn't speak.

The next day, the fourteenth of February, 1968, will stand out in my mind for as long as I live. It was then that we were interrogated the first time. I had been wondering when it would happen, when they would start trying to get information from us.

Hooknose was the interrogator, and he spoke English fairly well. He seemed to be proud of his position as interrogator.

"Have you had a pleasant walk?" he asked sarcastically. "Have you been treated well?"

"No, we haven't been treated well," I answered. "Our shoes were taken from us, our hands were tied behind our backs so we couldn't push the branches out of the way, we are in need of medical attention, and no one has told me what happened to Pfc. James George."

"Yes, well, we'll go to all of that later," Hooknose said, waving his hand impatiently. "First, I need the answers to a few questions."

"You must know that I have no intention of answering any of your questions," I replied.

Hooknose smiled and shook his head. "Don't worry,

there are just a few routine questions . . . questions to help the Red Cross inform your government and your family that you are alive and a prisoner of war."

"Oh," I said. "It would be good for my government and my family to get word."

Hooknose smiled. "Good, good, then you won't mind answering the questions. First your name."

"Benjamin H. Purcell."

"Your rank?"

"Lieutenant colonel."

"Your service number?"

"061035."

"What unit were you with when you were captured?"

"I can't tell you that."

"What was your position?"

"I can't tell you that, either."

"They are just routine questions."

"They are questions I can't answer."

"How many men in your unit?"

"Benjamin H. Purcell, lieutenant colonel, 061035."

Hooknose sighed and slapped his pencil down hard on the table.

"Don't you want your government informed? Don't you want your family to know you are alive?"

"Yes."

"How do you expect us to tell them you are a prisoner if you don't cooperate?"

"I'm giving you all the cooperation that's required by the Geneva Convention."

Hooknose smiled. "Well, you see then, there is the problem. We didn't sign the Geneva Convention." He turned to Mr. Rose. "You," he said. "Perhaps you will be more cooperative?"

"You aren't going to get any more out of me than you got from the colonel," Rose said defiantly.

"You will not talk to us?"

"I'll give you my name, rank, service number, and date of birth. That's all."

Hooknose turned to one of the other guards. He said something in Vietnamese and the guard reached for Mr. Rose.

"I have ordered this man executed," Hooknose said. "Perhaps after one of you is shot, the others will cooperate."

"You have no right to do that," I protested angrily.

"I have the guns, you know. I can do anything I wish." Hooknose nodded his head and Rose was taken away. I could see the fear in his eyes, but he gritted his teeth and said nothing.

"Colonel, are they really going to shoot him?" Chenoweth asked.

"I don't know," I answered truthfully.

"What are we going to do?"

"We are going to be soldiers," I replied.

We waited for a long, anxious moment but didn't hear a shot. After a short while the guards came for another prisoner, this time Chenoweth. Again I listened for a shot, but again I heard nothing. Lenker and I remained seated on the stick bed . . . but not for long.

Two guards approached and pulled me to the center of the cabin to the edge of a hole. I stood on the edge and looked down into the black pit. Was this to be my grave?

"Now, we will talk," Hooknose said.

"You won't get any more from me now than you did before," I said.

"I can understand before. You are a colonel, you did not want to talk before your men. But the others will not hear you from over here. It is okay. They will not know you have talked."

"I'm not going to talk."

I heard one of the guards cock his rifle, and the metallic sound of the bolt shoving a shell into the chamber sent shivers down my spine. Still, I was determined that I wasn't going to talk.

"*Khom,*" Hooknose said to the guard. I knew that meant "no."

The guard said something in an angry, threatening voice, but Hooknose spoke back to him, just as angrily. They argued for a moment longer; then the guard turned and walked away.

"He wants to shoot you," Hooknose explained. "The

American bombing has killed his entire family and he hates Americans. I told him you are a prisoner and we must not shoot you."

"Thanks," I said.

"I don't know. Maybe he will not listen to me much longer if you do not cooperate."

Suddenly I realized what he was doing and I almost smiled. It was the old "good guy, bad guy" routine.

"Are you married?" Hooknose asked, almost conversationally.

"Yes."

"What is your wife's name?"

I hesitated for a long moment, then I decided that his having Anne's name might help in getting information to her.

"My wife's name is Anne Purcell," I said.

"Where does she live?"

Again, I measured the weight of my response. I couldn't see that telling them where she lived would give them any strategic information. On the other hand, that specific knowledge might help in getting information to her.

"She lives in Boonville, Missouri," I said.

Hooknose smiled. "Well, now, you said you would give us no more information, but you gave us your wife's name and told us where she lives. That wasn't too hard was it?" Hooknose asked. "A little more information here, a little more there, and soon you'll understand how easy it is to tell us everything we need to know."

For Hooknose it was a great psychological victory. My cheeks burned with shame. I had violated the code only to the degree that I added my wife's name and address to the information I was authorized and required to give. At the moment it had seemed all right to me because the Geneva Convention on Land Warfare provides for POWs to write their next of kin. How can one do that without giving their name and address? Perhaps that was a rationalization, but I desperately wanted Anne to know that I was alive and well. However, as Hooknose pointed out to me, this was the first chink in the armor of the code. Was he right? And if one came right down to it, was I still bound by the code? I had already broken it by surrendering the men under my command.

"Why are you in Vietnam?" Hooknose suddenly asked.

"Because I'm a career soldier," I answered.

"That's the only reason? Because you are a career soldier? You could be a mercenary."

"No, that isn't the only reason. I volunteered to come to Vietnam because I believe in what I'm doing."

"You believe in killing women and children who are fighting for their freedom?"

"I believe in helping the Vietnamese people determine their own destiny," I said.

Hooknose laughed, but it wasn't a laugh of humor; it was more a laugh of scorn.

"That is funny," he said. "Coming from any American it is funny, but coming from you makes it very funny."

I was confused by his statement and I told him so.

"You say you want the Vietnamese people to determine their own destiny?"

"Yes. What makes that funny?"

"It is funny because you are with the CIA."

Now it was my time to laugh.

"Why do you laugh?"

"Why do you call me CIA?"

"We know who you are."

"I am Lieutenant Colonel Benjamin H. Purcell, U.S. Army."

"If you really are in the army, you can give me more information than you have."

"No, I can't. You know I can give you nothing but my name, rank, service number, and date of birth."

"You have already done more than that," Hooknose said. "You have not only told me the name of your wife, you have also told me where she lives."

"Yes, but I will tell you no more than that."

"The others who were with you have given more information. Much more."

"I don't believe that."

"How do you think we found out you are with the CIA?"

"You haven't found out because it isn't true."

"Who are you?"

"Purcell, Benjamin H., lieutenant colonel, service number 061035."

"Enough of that!" Hooknose suddenly shouted, and perhaps to show that he was tired of playing the good guy, bad guy routine, he backhanded me. I had gone through so much over the past week—the broken ribs, the swollen feet and legs, the hours of agonizing marching—that I barely felt his blow.

"Take off your clothes," he suddenly said.

"Why do you want me to take off my clothes?"

"You will be given other clothes to wear—fresh, clean clothes."

My uniform was dirty, smelly, and itching. But it was still the uniform of the U.S. Army. They had already taken my boots, billfold, ID cards, photographs, watch, and rings, but I still had my uniform. Despite the appeal of clean, fresh clothes, I had no desire to give up my uniform. I hesitated.

"Do you need help?" Hooknose asked.

I knew they were going to take my uniform with or without my cooperation, so I sighed and began unbuttoning my fatigue jacket.

Now that they were taking my uniform, I felt as if I were being stripped of more than just clothes—I was being stripped of my humanity. Then a funny thing happened. As I was stepping out of my trousers, I had a sudden revelation. I knew that the uniform was just the outside trappings. My real humanity was my soul, and there was nothing these people could do, even including killing me, that could reach my soul. That thought comforted me, and I took off my uniform without further protest.

"Here," Hooknose said. He handed me a pair of black cotton trousers and a shirt. They looked like pajamas. "You will like this better, I think."

This was the ubiquitous uniform of all Vietnamese—North and South, man and woman, peasant and revolutionary. I took them from him.

"Yes, I'm sure I will," I answered, but my sarcasm was lost on him.

A moment later I had the pajamas on while my uniform, the last vestige of my previous life, lay in a heap at my feet.

"Ah, good," Hooknose said. He looked at me and laughed scornfully. "Now you look the way you should," he said. He waved his arm toward one of the guards and said something in Vietnamese. The guard came over to grab me.

"There," the guard said pointing to the hole. "You go there."

I crawled down into the hole, sat down, and surveyed my new surroundings. It was cold, damp and cramped in the three-foot cube dug there in the floor of that cabin. Rocks protruding from the wall added to my discomfort.

I leaned back against the side of the hole trying to find a position that was halfway comfortable, but the space was too cramped. I was cold, hungry, and despondent. I was suffering from blistered feet and broken ribs. In short, I was miserable.

Suddenly I realized that it was the fourteenth of February and my fortieth birthday. I'd always heard that "life begins at forty," but I thought, "Lord, I'd just as soon stay thirty-nine if life after forty is going to be anything like this."

Thinking of the irony of it, I laughed out loud. Hooknose heard me laugh and came back over to look down in the hole at me.

"Why do you laugh?" he asked.

"I'm forty years old today," I said. I started to tell him about the "life begins at forty" part, but realized he wouldn't understand.

"Today is your birthday?"

"Yes."

"It is a special day for you?"

"I suppose it is," I said. "I'll say this for it. I've never spent a birthday quite like this one."

"It's your fault for coming to make war on my country," Hooknose said. He walked away from me then, leaving me in the hole, watched over by one of the armed guards.

I recalled my birthday the year before and the strawberry cake with thirty-nine candles. I thought of a wedge of it on a plate before me, moist and rich, covered with a creamy strawberry icing. I wondered if thinking about it was making things easier or harder.

I got angry with myself then for feeling sorry for myself. After all, we don't choose life; we must accept it one day at a time and live each day to its fullest.

I stayed in that hole for six or seven hours and then had to go outside to the toilet. As I hobbled back into the hut I found an egg the hen had just laid. I picked it up and handed it to Hooknose. Specialist Lenker was sitting on the dirt floor by a small fire so I sat on the ground beside him to get warm. We talked for a while, and then I dozed off for a few minutes' sleep. Sometime later Lenker shook me and said, "Colonel, supper's ready." When I sat up, I saw Hooknose standing over me holding a small metal plate. He handed it to me.

"What is this?" I asked, surprised by the gesture.

"It is your birthday?"

"Yes."

"It is the custom of the Vietnamese people to remember the special days in the lives of those who are guests in their homes, and although you are not a guest in this man's home, he knows it is your birthday and wants to honor it with the only thing he has to offer you. Here is an egg for your supper."

I looked over at the Montagnard. He bowed and smiled.

"Why, I . . . I thank you," I said, touched very deeply by his gesture. I regarded what the man had done for me as a real symbol of humanity. I was sure that God had used this Montagnard to show me that he was with me, even in prison, and I was greatly encouraged.

That Montagnard wasn't a soldier, and I wasn't his enemy. We were merely two human beings caught up in events, and this was a moment of sharing. I was twelve thousand miles from home, and we were very different politically, economically, educationally—almost any way you want to compare human beings. His act of kindness transcended our differences and helped me realize that all people strive for essentially the same things: for peace, for freedom, and for an opportunity to work, to love, and to be loved. Looking back, I see that in a way my life did begin anew at forty, because I now look at humanity through a different pair of eyes.

The next morning, Rose and Chenoweth rejoined Lenker and me. I believe Hooknose had been trying to break each of us individually by separating us for the one night. He did not succeed.

We were told to get ready to move. Though it was tough going for them, Rose, Chenoweth, and Lenker were at least able to walk, but I could no longer even stand on my raw feet as we prepared to leave the cabin.

Hooknose sent a guard to a nearby hut, where Rose had spent the night. There were several prisoners there from the ARVN, and Hooknose impressed four of them into service as litter bearers. I was placed in a blanket, which was then suspended from a single pole. With two ARVN prisoners on each end of the pole we started out. Stoic and uncomplaining, those four young Vietnamese soldiers carried me through the jungle for the better part of that day.

Near nightfall we arrived at a new jungle camp. The perimeter fence was nothing but strips of bamboo woven in a crosshatch pattern. A single guard was stationed at the only entrance to the compound. There was one hut at the entrance and two more were inside, one much larger than the other. The four of us were placed in the larger hut. Apparently there was at least one other prisoner in the smaller hut.

Two days after we arrived in this new camp we heard a familiar voice. It was Warrant Officer Ziegler! I had mixed feelings: I was glad he was alive but sorry he hadn't made it back to safety. Dick was placed in the smaller hut. We were not permitted to communicate with him directly, but we soon found out that whenever we were summoned to the camp headquarters, we could walk close enough to his hut to exchange a few words.

Ziegler told us he had evaded capture for about twenty-four hours after getting out of the shell crater but had been unable to make the journey back to the friendly unit at Quang Tri because of the bullet wound in his leg. After capture he received rudimentary medical care in a first-aid station before walking to the present camp. He also told us that the other person in the hut with him was an American named King David Rayford.

Rayford had been a prisoner for ten months already, mostly in this compound by himself. He told us that he had been captured in the city of Hue in May of 1967. He had been a driver for one of the truck companies attached to my old command. One day as he was driving through the city of Hue with a load of supplies, he decided to spend half an hour in town for a little R & R.

Rayford instructed his assistant driver to deliver the supplies and return for him in about thirty minutes. He had walked alone for only a short distance before a Viet Cong suddenly appeared, pointed a pistol at his head and demanded that he surrender. What a way to lose one's freedom.

At this new camp we were fed two meals each day consisting of boiled rice with a few chunks of cassava root mixed in. The four of us in the larger hut received one canteen of water with each meal, which was never enough to satisfy our thirsty.

There was always a fire burning in the hut, so sometimes to alter the flavor of our food we would take the cassava root from the rice and roast it in the fire until it was as black as charcoal. The burned cassava had a different taste from the white boiled root. Besides, we believed the charred root would help stem the diarrhea that plagued us all.

At this jungle camp I received the first medical attention for my blistered feet and cracked ribs. Once, and only once, an aid man dusted some white powder on the soles of my feet and wrapped them with gauze. The treatment for my rib was unusual. First the medic inserted a hypodermic needle into my right rib cage—I believe he was trying to reduce the swelling by drawing out the fluid. Next he placed a bamboo splint over my ribs and bandaged my chest. Then he strapped my right arm to my side. After ten days the bandage was removed, and although the ribs felt better, my shoulder was almost frozen in its socket.

Around the first of March there was quite a commotion in our camp. The camp officials were very upset because Dick and King had disappeared during the night. Dick later told us they had simply walked out of the camp after dark when the guards relaxed their vigil. The night had been so dark that they had navigated by the flashes of fireflies, moving a few feet with each flash. Still they had bumped into trees so often that they had decided to stop moving until daylight. They had begun walking again at daybreak but had run into a VC search party at noon and had been returned to the compound.

As punishment Dick spent a week in a hole dug under King's bed, and his meager rations were cut in half. We never found out why King was not punished. Perhaps the camp commander thought Dick had coerced him into escaping.

Around mid-March we six Americans departed the camp in the custody of Hooknose and six guards. The guards carried all their personal belongings on their backs, including hens in bamboo cages.

For nine days we walked over mountains and across river bottoms in the northwestern part of South Vietnam. At times the exertion was too much for Chenoweth and he would turn ghostly white and pass out. Twice I picked him up and carried him on my back for a few hundred yards until he recovered his strength. Rayford did the same several more times.

Drinking water was always in short supply on the trail. We started each day with one canteen full of previously boiled water—yes, there was only one among us—but with six thirsty Americans drinking from the same canteen the supply was quickly exhausted. Our guards routinely denied us the opportunity to drink water directly from the streams. However, on one occasion I ignored their directions and scooped up some water in my hand. It tasted cool and sweet, but by nightfall I realized what an unwise thing I had done. I spent most of that night squatting over a slit trench.

Another day the group stopped near a mountaintop for a brief rest and to boil some more water for drinking. While the water boiled, Hooknose took an egg one of the hens had laid earlier that morning and put it in the pot. Several minutes later he retrieved the egg and handed it to me.

"This is for you," he said. "Not because you are a colonel but because you are an old man."

I was older than the other POWs, I admit, and I was older than any of the VC guards. But I had never actually considered myself an old man before. Nevertheless, I took the egg.

In addition to the shortage of drinking water and the fatigue we experienced on this nine-day journey, we were also
plagued with the ever-present leeches. Those slimy creatures
would latch onto our ankles, legs, or torsos and feast on our
blood. There was no pain associated with the leech bite,
which really wasn't a bite at all but an incising and sucking
process. However, a small bleeding wound in that climate became very susceptible to infection. During the nine days on
the trail, 127 Vietnamese leeches, by actual count, sucked my
blood.

Around dusk each day we would stop to make camp.
This was a simple process since we had no personal belongings and no tents to erect. First we would gather dead wood
and start a fire, over which the guards would boil water and
cook rice for our meal. Guards and prisoners ate out of the
same pot.

The shelter for the night for the six Americans was one
poncho suspended between trees or bushes. On rainy nights
we would alternate positions every two hours to allow the two
outer persons an opportunity to lie in the middle, where it
was relatively drier. We soon learned that when six men get
close enough together to share one poncho there has to be a
high degree of cooperation. One also quickly learns to share
the misery with his fellow man, as well as any good thing that
may come along, however small. One example was the banana I found on the ground as we passed through a grove of
banana plants. It was very small, only about three inches
long, but we split it six ways. All any of us got was a good
smell.

At the end of our nine-day journey we stopped at a camp
that was more organized than any of the previous ones. It
appeared to be a staging area of sorts for possible later
moves. I sensed there was soon to be a drastic change in our
situation and even entertained the idea that the war had
ended and we were on our way to a release point. Hope was
still alive!

When I left our hut to go to the toilet the next morning,
I saw a pile of trash nearby. Something shiny in the trash pile
caught my attention, and I walked over to investigate. There
in the trash I found one of my dogtags. I was surprised and

a little confused as to how it got here. As I was about to leave, I noticed another dogtag. When I picked it up, I saw that it belonged to Pfc. James George!

I felt a surge of elation! If George's dogtag was here with mine, then Armband had told me the truth. They had gotten him a doctor and he was still alive. Maybe he was here in this very camp. What a wonderful prospect that was!

When I went back inside, I felt much better. Nothing had really changed. I was still a prisoner of war and had no idea how long I would be. But now I could hang onto the hope that George was alive and being treated somewhere for his injuries.

I had been a prisoner for more than a month now, and my thoughts were constantly with Anne and the children. Were they all right? Did they know of my situation? I desperately wanted to write to Anne, but the VC refused all requests. Nevertheless, I wrote a letter every day in my mind.

I also thought about my room back in Da Nang. If I had been rational about it, I would have realized that it had undoubtedly been cleaned out by then, probably for my replacement. But it comforted me to think of it just as I had left it, as if at any moment I could go back and resume my life exactly where it had been interrupted by the downing of our helicopter.

The room was air-conditioned, with clean sheets and bookshelves loaded with books. There I had the family picture we had taken just before I left home. I could close my eyes and see that picture. Better than that, I could close my eyes and bring each member of my family to mind—Anne, David, Debbie, Cliff, Sherri, and Joy. I knew that Joy was too young to remember me. . . . I hoped the others wouldn't forget.

Then I began to worry. What if they never let me write a letter? What if they really did believe I was with the CIA? I no longer was so sure Armband had been playing games with me. I started to entertain the idea that he thought I was a spy. If he told Hooknose that, and the others began believing it, they might not feel that it was necessary to treat me as a prisoner of war. And then not only could they very well refuse me permission to write or hear from my family, they might even withhold information from my government and my family about my status.

No, I told myself. No, I couldn't let negative thoughts enter my mind. If they weren't going to let me write, I'd just have to deal with it somehow. I simply would not dwell on the possibility that God would give me a greater burden than I could carry.

Anyway, I told myself, it wasn't necessary that I actually write to communicate with Anne. I had been writing letters daily in my heart and somehow I knew she was receiving them—if not in fact then in spirit. She may not have known exactly what I was saying, but she did know of my love for her. She had to.

"Anne," I said quietly, "whatever you know or don't know, be brave. Find solace and strength in the Lord and in my love. If you do that, we won't be apart. Not really."

6

MOVING TO BAO CAO

A change in our status had occurred, as I had suspected, but unfortunately it was not a prelude to our release. Instead, I realized with a sense of despair, we were now somewhere in the countryside of North Vietnam. That was very significant to me. All the time we were in South Vietnam there was always the hope, no matter how dim, that we might encounter an American patrol. But there were no American ground troops in North Vietnam, so even that remote hope was now denied.

Our guards were changed again. Hooknose and his group turned us over to a new relief. This group of guards was led by someone I called Goldtooth. Goldtooth could speak better English than Armband or Hooknose, but other than our being able to communicate a little better there was no noticeable change in our situation.

Late on March 31 the six of us were moved to a point where we waited until nightfall. We must have been somewhere in the upper portion of the Ashau Valley near the Laotian border. There was evidence of a great deal of vehicular traffic on this crudely constructed road, which was actually little more than a clearing of trees along a trail.

As we waited, the sound of approaching trucks became louder by the minute. Before long a medium-sized truck—I would compare it to an American 2½-ton—stopped along the road just a few yards from where our group was waiting. The driver knew exactly where to stop even though we were concealed by the undergrowth of trees.

Goldtooth and his men ordered us to load up, and thus began the roughest, most uncomfortable motor trip of my life. The truck seemed to have no shocks or springs, there were no seats—just the hard metal floor—and by now we had all lost so many pounds that there was no padding on our rear ends to cushion the shock. As the old joke says, the driver knew where all the potholes were and managed to hit every one of them. We ran over rocks that were too large for a bulldozer to push out of the way, and we wallowed through great sloughs of mud filled with logs. Mile after miserable mile, hour after endless hour, we lurched and bounced along this road, the name of which was as recognizable to Americans as the Pennsylvania Turnpike.

This torturous, pathetic road was a part of the labyrinth known as the Ho Chi Minh Trail which trespassed through the eastern part of Laos.

At daybreak following the first night's ride, the truck halted at what appeared to be a huge field hospital. Here, a number of tents and makeshift huts were scattered across an area of several acres. We saw hundreds of wounded North Vietnamese soldiers with bandaged heads, arms, legs, and torsos. There were so many of them out in the open that I thought of that famous scene in the movie *Gone with the Wind,* in which thousands of wounded soldiers are lying on the ground at the Atlanta Depot. These men were enemy soldiers, and yet combat wounds were a badge of honor recognized by fighting men everywhere. In an odd way I felt a type of kinship . . . a brotherhood of arms, as it were, with these men who had shared the same dangers as we, albeit on the opposite side of the war.

We remained at the hospital all that day. At some point our group was fed the first really hot meal we had received in almost two months. We each had a very small piece of meat (we wondered if it was water buffalo), boiled rice, and a leafy green vegetable. We also received a cup of hot beverage, which may have been some sort of tea. Compared to the other meals we had been receiving this was like a feast.

At dusk our group was moved back to the truck, where we were joined by seven other prisoners: two Americans, two Philippine nationals, and three ARVN soldiers. One of the Americans was Captain Ted Gostas, the other, Master Sergeant John Anderson. We soon became well acquainted and developed a mutual trust, the kind of trust that is necessary for survival in a prisoner-of-war situation.

Captain Gostas had been serving in Hue as an advisor to the Vietnamese police chief. He was captured during the Tet offensive. Master Sergeant Anderson was working at the American armed forces radio station just outside Hue when the station was overrun and all personnel were captured. Two other radio-station personnel were captured—the two Filipinos, who had been employed as mechanics at the radio station. One we called Art and the other Pop. They were both very friendly and supportive of group needs, sharing with us their meager possessions and helping us adjust to the strange jungle environment of Eastern Laos.

Since I could not speak Vietnamese I never found out much about the ARVN prisoners, but I suspected they were even more concerned about their personal welfare and future than we Americans were. I had already learned that the ARVNs were frequently considered traitors rather than prisoners of war.

After another night of bouncing along the Ho Chi Minh Trail, we stopped at dawn and unloaded. There were thirteen of us prisoners now. We were herded along a narrow trail through bamboo thickets for about two miles until we came to a small lean-to, where we were allowed to get some sleep. Twice during that day we were served a meal of rice balls and hot water. That may not seem like a very appetizing menu, but to men as hungry as we were it was a welcome event.

During the late afternoon, Art, one of the Filipino prisoners, noticed my sore bare feet and offered to help. Borrowing a machete from one of the guards, he used it to cut up a small burlap bag he had been using to carry his blanket and extra pair of trousers. After a few deft strokes, he had the basic outline of a pair of, for want of a better description, booties, which he meticulously but very gently measured to my feet. When he was satisfied with the fit, Art tied the boo-ties in place with strips of scrap burlap. I cannot describe what a blessing it was to have something between the soles of my feet and the rocky ground. Art's booties nearly grew to my feet over the remaining seven days of our journey, but they saved me a great deal of pain.

We didn't ride very far on the ninth day. We soon arrived at a point within walking distance of a prisoner-of-war com-pound near the city of Vinh, North Vietnam.

There was a subtle difference in the mood of the Viet-namese guards we encountered here. Whereas before we had been with guards who were sharing the rigors of our journey, these men were reception personnel. Over the years I had observed within our own army how reception personnel, faced with transients day in and day out, sometimes allowed the frustrations of their jobs to spill over to their treatment of men who were just "passing through." That same attitude existed here, only we weren't replacement troops from their own army—we were prisoners of war.

We were ordered to unload and sit down. I could manage fine whenever I was either sitting or walking, but the transi-tion from a sitting to a standing position was sheer agony. By now my legs were covered with infected sores resulting from the untreated leech bites. Malnutrition, the forced marches, diarrhea, and infections were taking a heavy toll on each of us. It was all I could do to make it down from the truck, and once I was on the ground I was sure I wouldn't be able to get up again.

After a brief rest we were told to get up and follow a guide. I delayed for a minute or two because of the intense pain in my legs. One of the headmen saw that I was holding up the movement and said something to one of the guards.

Ted, who could understand some Vietnamese, whispered to me.

"Colonel, you'd better get up and get moving," he said. "The headman just told the guard to shoot you if you don't get going right away."

Since the headman hadn't said anything to me, but

merely passed the order along quietly, almost routinely, to the guard, I realized that this was no threat for the purpose of frightening me. This was for real! I learned then that a person can do difficult or even impossible tasks when the adrenaline flows from excitement or fear. Despite the pain I got moving right away.

It was exceptionally dark that night and I couldn't see to walk. For several minutes I stumbled along, tripping over unseen roots and rocks. Each ditch or rut in the road was a major obstacle. I felt tired, beaten, and almost helpless. I already knew that if I fell I was going to be shot. I was no longer the self-sufficient and supremely confident infantry officer I had been two months earlier. I needed help, and I asked for it in the simple prayer of a man who was on his last legs. I didn't couch my needs in a prayer for the strength to bear what he had given me or for the power of spirit to love my enemies or for the gift of serenity. I needed a light and that's exactly what I asked for.

"Lord, I've got to have a light here, because I cannot see to walk and I'm not going to survive this march unless I can keep up with the others."

I will always believe that what happened next was a miracle—in the overall scheme of things, a small one, perhaps, but for me a lifesaver. Within sixty seconds the guide, who until now had been content to walk in the darkness, suddenly turned on a flashlight and directed the beam right at my feet. He kept it there for the remainder of the night. Never before had God answered my prayer so dramatically and so soon.

We reached a camp I called Bao Cao. That's my name for it; I don't know how the Vietnamese referred to it. I called it Bao Cao because it was here we were first instructed to bow and say *bao cao* if we had any requests to make of the camp cadre. I really don't know what it means, but I presumed that *bao cao* was similar to our word "please." I used the word routinely when asking for food, medicine, blankets, and so on . . . but I absolutely refused to bow. To me it was important to be courteous but not subservient in my relationship with the cadre.

It was here that I suffered the greatest blow since my capture. Despite all my protests, the other prisoners were taken away and I was left alone. The next few days were the most depressing I had ever experienced. Even though we had been able to communicate only in whispers, we had at least been able to communicate. Even more importantly, we had been able to see one another and drew strength from the others' presence. I don't think I ever realized what a gregarious fellow I was until my companions were taken from me. The silence was deafening!

In those first few hours of enforced solitude, I recalled something Bishop Fulton J. Sheen once said: "A man who cannot live with himself cannot live with his fellow man." That was the situation I found myself in. I was forced to live by myself. I figured I was going to get to know myself pretty well before all this was over.

My world now consisted of the compound and my cell. There wasn't much to the compound. The best thing to say about it was that it was primitive. It consisted of one building eight cells long, built half underground. The roof was straw and sod, and the building was surrounded by a drainage ditch and barbed wire. There were at least two more Americans there, but I was prohibited from having any contact with them. There was an outdoor toilet, and a stream was nearby. They allowed us to take a bath once a week, which I did by hobbling down to the stream and splashing water on myself. We were given a bar of lye soap, both for bathing and washing clothes. When the guard gave me a bar, he said it was to last for forty-five days.

I was in cell number one. It was a very small room, only three feet wide by seven feet long, with leg stocks built in at one end. It's funny, I used to have the image of prisoners pacing back and forth in their cells much like the animals I saw in the Atlanta Zoo when I was a child. I was sorry for the animals then. But as I think back on it, they were well-fed, got plenty of fresh air, and had others of their kind with them. They even had visitors almost every day. I would gladly have changed places with them.

I began to fear that I might lose one or both of my legs. They were covered with boils and open sores resulting from all those leech bites. Serious infection had set in, and I was afraid that blood poisoning would follow. I brought it up to Pugnose. "Pugnose" was the name I had given my newly assigned interrogator.

"I need a doctor, a *bac si*." I pointed to my legs, to the boils and sores and the little red lines of infection.

"No. No *bac si* until you talk. First you answer questions, then we take care of your needs . . . medicine, clothing, food. All will be nice for you then."

"You know I can't tell you any more than I already have," I said.

"You have no choice," Pugnose said. "You will answer our questions or you will lose your legs. Do you wish to go back home half a man? Of course," he added, smiling at me, "maybe you won't go back home at all. Maybe you will die here. Or maybe you won't die, but you will stay here, even when the war is over and all the prisoners are exchanged."

"How can you do that?"

"It would be very easy. We will charge you with crimes against the Vietnamese people."

"I have committed no crimes against the Vietnamese people," I said.

"You are committing a crime by not telling us what we want to know," Pugnose insisted. "You are not showing the proper attitude. You have not refirmed your thinking. Return to your cell for some self-appraisal. When you are ready to talk, I will see to it that you get some medicine for your legs."

I returned to my cell and thought about the situation for a long time. It had been almost three months since I was captured. Any tactical information I had was of no use to them now, but I knew I should resist giving them any item of information, however insignificant it may have seemed.

One might think that to lie would be a simple decision to make, but it wasn't. First there was the moral question. All right, I could satisfy that question by saying it wasn't really morally wrong to tell lies to your enemies if by telling them the truth you might cause harm to your country. But there was also the Code of Conduct. Was this another chink in the armor of the code? The code does not say tell lies; it says give only name, rank, service number, and date of birth.

I remembered a discussion at Fort Benning, Georgia,

one Saturday morning. I was getting ready to give a TI & E (troop information and education) class when the subject of the Code of Conduct came up.

"Why can't a prisoner of war just lie when he is asked questions?" somebody wanted to know.

The textbook answer was, "Because even by lying, one could inadvertently give the enemy information."

The funny thing about that discussion was, I couldn't remember which side of the question I had been on. Had I been one of those who thought you should be able to lie? Or had I been one of the strict interpreters of the law, insisting that you aren't authorized to lie—that you should give only name, rank, service number, and date of birth?

Whichever side of the question I was on then, I now came to the conclusion that it was better to lie than to face the possibility of losing my legs through deliberate nontreatment. I made a conscious decision to depart from my lifelong ethic of truthfulness in order to deceive the enemy. I finally called for a guard and asked to be taken to Pugnose.

Pugnose was sitting behind a little table with a smug expression on his face. I had already determined that I was going to tell him some lies, but seeing his expression almost made me change my mind. I didn't want to give him the satisfaction of even thinking he had broken me. However, there was still the problem of my legs.

"So, you are now ready to answer a few questions?"

"Yes," I said quietly.

"I did not hear you."

"Yes," I said louder.

"Good, good, very good," Pugnose said. "Ah, won't you have some tea?" He waved his hand and one of the guards came over to pour a cup of tea for me. Except for the one meal at the field hospital, I had drunk nothing but warm water for three months. The thought of a cup of tea actually made me salivate, and I was angry with myself for such a reaction. My hands were trembling when I took the first taste. It was strong and there was a slight metallic taste to it . . . but it was delicious.

"Now . . . what was your job?"

"I was the troop information and education officer," I

said. That wasn't entirely a lie. As a deputy commander of a sub-area, I had several collateral duties, and TI & E was one of them. I knew that the North Vietnamese army, indeed all of the Communist armies, had political officers who were a very important part of their command structure. Because that was their experience, I figured Pugnose would believe me.

"Ah," he said, smiling broadly. Pugnose did believe me. "Tell me, how many soldiers were you responsible for?"

"About two hundred," I answered. I pulled the number out of my hat. It didn't mean anything.

"What was the nature of your duties?"

"To provide the soldiers with information," I said. "For example, in one of the last classes I conducted we discussed the advantages of a zone defense over a man-to-man."

That wasn't actually a lie either. Because the MPs had given a number of traffic citations to our drivers, I called several of them together to discuss driving safety. We had just watched the film of a football game the night before, and someone started talking about the zone defense used by the Baltimore Colts. Someone else suggested that a really good quarterback, someone like Joe Namath, could pick a zone defense apart. The only chance to defend against someone like Namath, they said, would be man-to-man.

"What is this zone and man-to-man defense?" Pugnose asked, certain that he had happened onto a vital piece of information.

I started talking about zone defense, throwing in every word I had ever heard a sportscaster say, even if I didn't know what it meant. I talked about safety blitzes, seams, red dogs, bump and go, zig out, zig in, post pattern, fly, flag pattern, linebacker drops, free safeties, and cornerbacks. Pugnose was writing everything down excitedly, sometimes asking me to spell something for him. Whenever he asked for an explanation, I would purposely make it more garbled while pretending to clarify it.

"What is a linebacker drop?" he asked.

"Well, say you've got an outside blitz on," I said. "If the corners blitz, then they leave a seam that can only be covered by a dropping linebacker. But if you do that, you've got to be very careful they don't come in under the coverage so the inside linebackers will have to stay in and cover not only the middle but outside as well. The outside linebackers can drop to the corner coverage area, and you'll have to count on the free safety to handle anything deep."

"The free safety?" Pugnose said writing it down carefully.

"Yes, or the monster man."

"What is the monster man?"

"That's a code for free safety."

Pugnose smiled and wagged his head happily. "Yes, yes, now this is good, you tell us the code. This is very good, these are the things we want. Monster man is free safety."

"For deep coverage," I told him.

He wrote down "deep coverage."

"Uh, listen," I said, looking around. "I wouldn't want it out that I told you all of this. I don't want the other Americans to hear about it."

"Don't worry," Pugnose said. "We will say nothing. When you return to your cell, you will find medicine for the sores on your legs. It will kill the infection and ease the pain."

"Thank you," I said.

"Take this," Pugnose said. He gave me a change of clothes.

"Thank you very much," I said again.

When I returned to my cell, a first-aid man came by and treated the sores on my legs. He gave me an injection and then dusted a white powder on each sore and wrapped the sores with gauze. The pain quickly subsided to a tolerable level.

I was still isolated from the other American prisoners. Not only could I not talk to them, I didn't even get to see them. I did hear a couple of them though. The screams of one of them haunted me in the night. It sounded like Captain Gostas's voice.

"Kill me!" he cried. "Kill me . . . go ahead and kill me!" It sounded to me as though they were trying to obtain information on who the undercover policemen were in the city of Hue. That convinced me that it was Captain Gostas who was being interrogated. The next day I asked Pugnose who it was and what was going on, but he wouldn't talk about it.

I had also heard another American calling out for water. It may have been that he was on a hunger strike and they were withholding water from him. I told Pugnose that they must give the American water, and shortly thereafter my countryman quit crying out. Whether it was because he ended his hunger strike or they acceded to my demand, I honestly didn't know.

7

MOVING TO COLUMBUS

When Ben received orders for his tour in Vietnam we gave much thought to where the children and I should live the year he would be gone. We decided it would be best for us to remain in Boonville. David was entering his first year of high school, and we felt that he shouldn't have to cope with any more changes at this time. In addition, the rest of the family liked Boonville, had friends there, and were happily settled.

With the situation now drastically changed and with no idea when, or *if,* Ben would return, I wondered what we should do. I was concerned about it from February through most of April, as we awaited the outcome of the war. I felt we should move closer to our relatives far away in Georgia. I spoke with Reverend Clemons and other friends about this question. They all had their suggestions, but the bottom line was it was a decision I would have to make for myself.

For all the years of our marriage Ben and I had decided the important things like this together. Now the burden was on my shoulders. I found myself repeatedly asking God, "Where should we live, what should we do?"

My mother and Ben's mom both suggested that we move to Clarkesville so that we would be close to them. In fact, there was a house right across from Mother's on Laurel Drive that was for rent or for sale. My emotions cried out, "Go there so you will be with family and they can help you." The responsibility for the children weighed heavily on my mind, and the suggestion that someone else might assume some of it tempted me to go to Clarkesville.

But one day in April as I again asked that question, "Where should we live, what should we do?" a voice suddenly spoke to me. It said, "Go to Columbus, Georgia, and wait." I was sure that was God's answer to me. He didn't waste any words; he got right to the point and spoke with authority. I felt that was exactly how God would speak. I was very comfortable with this answer and began to make plans for our move.

Ben had had a tour of duty at Fort Benning in the late 1950s. We had purchased a house then, but at the time of Ben's capture it was rented to a military family. Mr. Bob Whitt, a Columbus neighbor, was the caretaker of our property, so I called and asked him to see about getting the renters to vacate our house by midsummer. This would allow us to move in before school started in September. Our plans were moving forward.

Not hearing from Ben left a void in my life. However, as friends heard what had happened they wrote or called, and these messages gave me a great deal of comfort. They told me that others cared and were getting in touch to let us know of their concern. This was an important lesson that I learned firsthand: to always show others you care even if words fail you. Just a hug, a caring look, a squeeze of the hand or a simple printed card means so much to one who is hurting.

I did not receive a letter from Ben's commanding officer about Ben's shoot-down until a month later. I felt he should have written sooner. However, a very good friend of Ben's at Da Nang, Chaplain Bagnal, wrote to me within just a few days after the crash. He told me as much as he knew about the shoot-down, and this was comforting to me. Just hearing from someone who had served with Ben in Vietnam was very special. I was glad he and Ben had had the chance to become friends, spend some time together talking about their families, and worship together in the Chapel of the Flags.

Chaplain Bagnal related that he had been planning to go on the February 8 flight with Ben, but when he had arrived to board the helicopter Ben had told him he was being bumped from the flight. A refrigeration mechanic was needed in Quang Tri to make some repairs on a disabled reefer truck and was to make the trip instead of the chaplain. How thankful I was that the chaplain's family had been spared what we were experiencing.

At the close of his letter Chaplain Bagnal related a funny story. As he was coming to the chapel one Sunday morning, he saw stalks of bananas growing on the recently planted banana trees in front of the chapel. He was shocked to see that they had grown so fast, but when he examined them more closely, he saw that the banana bunches had been tied to the trees. Then he heard Ben, Colonel Pierce, and Sergeant Duffy laughing behind him and realized who was responsible for the joke.

I hoped Ben would now find something funny to make him laugh.

8

BRAINWASHING AT

K-77

BEN'S STORY

I was becoming obsessed with the idea of writing a letter to Anne, but no matter how often I asked I was denied the opportunity. So I wrote this letter to her anyway, inscribing it in my heart.

Somewhere in Vietnam
May 1, 1968

My Darling Anne,
I have to confess that I am having a very difficult time
with depression right now. And yet, depressed as I am, I
can't imagine how things are going for you back in
Boonville. You have the total responsibility of the family on
your shoulders. And whereas I know you are safe, you have
no idea about my situation. In many ways life has to be

*more difficult for you than for me. No doubt you are
depressed enough without having to experience my
depression as well.*

*I know, I know, that probably sounds funny. After all,
this isn't a real letter in the sense that it isn't actually being
sent to you. So any bout with depression I might have, even
if I shared it in these thoughts, would still be my own.*

*But I don't look at it that way, Anne. I look at this as
an actual letter, and I feel it in my heart, because I must feel
that you are receiving it. Therefore, when I am most
depressed, I can't make myself compose one of them. Please
understand.*

*Soon it will be Debbie's eleventh birthday. She is such a
beautiful and energetic young lady and always seems to find
the "roses among the thorns of life." Please make her special
day the very best you can and give her an extra tight hug for
me. I love her very much.*

*Speaking of birthdays, Sweetheart, you have one
coming up a week after Debbie's, so I want to wish you a
happy birthday too. Maybe the two of you can have a party
together. I honestly do not know what gift I would have
gotten you had I not been captured, but right now you'd
probably be happy just to have me home.*

*My love to you always, and to all of our children. Good
night. I love you, and I'm not mad at you.*

YOURS FOREVER, BEN

Late in the afternoon of July 3 a guard called me out of
my cell to give me a haircut. He used the old-style hand clip-
pers that pulled more hair out than it cut. He then gave me
a canvas duffle bag and told me, "Pack your things. You will
be moved to a new location tonight."

After dark our cell doors were opened and we three prisoners were told, "Follow the guide but do not talk." I immediately recognized Captain Ted Gostas and later learned that
the third person was an army sergeant, Dennis Thompson.
Dennis appeared to be in reasonably good health, but Ted's
right arm hung by his side in a strange manner. Could this be
evidence that he had been tortured several weeks before?

We were instructed to stay about fifteen yards apart as we started to walk along a narrow dirt path. Up ahead I could see a much larger group of about sixteen prisoners walking single file as we were, and I assumed they too were Americans.

We walked all night, stopping briefly only twice. As the sun came up on our Independence Day, I saw the larger group being herded into a building that appeared to be a school or an abandoned church. Dennis, Ted, and I were moved into a thick patch of bamboo to await the return of darkness. To my surprise there was one other prisoner already in the bamboo patch. His name was Jim Thompson.

When we were served our first meal of the day, I found an excuse to move close to Jim, and we exchanged personal data. He told me he was an army Special Forces captain who had been shot down in late March 1964. I was stunned, for this man had already been a prisoner for more than four years. How many more Independence Days would come and go before we would again be free men? No one knew.

We walked for another night and then were loaded on vehicles for two more nights of travel. Sometime around midnight on the seventh of July we arrived at a rather large and permanent prison that I called K-77 because I saw the letter and numeral combination on several issues of a propaganda news letter which was circulated among the prisoners and assumed it was for identification of our prison. This camp was much better than Bao Cao, so I felt pretty good about the move. Here I had a wooden-slatted bed and a toilet bucket in my cell. To me this was a real convenience.

Apparently this compound was build by the French during the years when France held control of all of Indochina. Although I wasn't sure of the exact distance, I believed it was fairly close to a major city. It was a rather large compound surrounded by a fourteen-foot-high wall topped with barbed wire and electric wire. A good high school pole vaulter could have gotten over it, and although I was never a pole vaulter, I must confess that a favorite fantasy of mine had me grabbing a pole and vaulting over the wall right in front of the startled guards.

I was in a room at one end of a long building on the

north side of the grounds. My building looked like a run-down motel unit. In addition to the motel-type building where I was housed there was a kitchen building, guards' quarters, and the commandant's house. The ground of the prison was hard-packed dirt, and chickens walked around scratching and pecking at whatever they could find.

The food improved. Until my arrival at K-77, I had subsisted for five months on a diet of boiled rice and warm water. Here I was given an occasional vegetable with the rice and, not too long after I arrived, a loaf of French bread. Two cups of hot water also arrived with each meal, truly a luxury.

However, nothing is without its price; and I had to pay for the luxury, for here the brainwashing began.

I knew that the constant questions weren't to get information. I was sure that by now they had discovered I was just blowing smoke with all my talk of the zone defense, and yet they said nothing about it. No, what they really wanted was the opportunity to break my will. They asked me several times to sign a confession of "crimes against the Vietnamese people."

The chief interrogator here was a man I called Crisco. I called him that because he was so slick when we talked. He was about 5'6", with a narrow face, a skinny neck, and bushy black hair.

Crisco's assistant was a man I called Spit. Spit chewed tobacco or betel nut all the time, so you can guess where he got his name.

"It really means nothing, you know," Crisco said to me during one of his interrogations. "If you would just confess your crimes you would be treated much, much better."

"Better? How?" I asked.

"You would be able to see the other Americans," Crisco said. "You have been a prisoner for several months and you have been kept in solitary confinement for the entire time. Wouldn't you like to see some other Americans? Wouldn't you like to have a roommate? Someone you could talk to?"

Second only to going home, Crisco had hit upon my greatest desire.

"Yes. Yes, I would very much like to see other Americans," I admitted.

The thought of seeing another American face, of talking to another American, made me dizzy with want. And yet I couldn't meet Crisco's terms because the price he was about to demand for it was much too dear.

Crisco grinned. "All you have to do is confess your crimes," he said.

"I have no crimes to confess," I told him.

"When you were home, didn't you confess your sins to a priest? You can just pretend that I am a priest."

"It isn't in my religion to confess my sins to a priest," I told him. "I have no priest in my religion . . . I'm not a Catholic. I'm a Protestant, a member of a Southern Baptist church."

"Oh? And what of the cross the guards have seen in your room?"

"The cross is a religious symbol for all Christians."

"It is important to you? This cross?"

I hesitated a moment before I answered. If I said yes, he might decide to take it away from me just for spite. If I said no, he would know I was lying, because if it wasn't important, why would I have made it in the first place?

"It comforts me to have it," I said.

Crisco looked at me for a moment, then he nodded.

"You may keep the cross," he said.

"Thank you."

"I want you to confess your crimes."

"Is that what I have to do to keep the cross? Because if it is I won't do it."

"No," Crisco said. "You may keep the cross."

Despite Crisco's assurances, when I returned to my cell I discovered that the cross was gone. While I was being interrogated, someone had entered my cell and taken it. I was very upset when I realized the cross was taken, but as I considered it I decided I didn't really need a bamboo cross to look at. All I actually needed was an abiding faith, and that I had.

My earlier belief that the food had greatly improved may have been a bit premature. I was served stewed pumpkins for twenty consecutive days. I never want to see another pumpkin again . . . and that includes pumpkin pie for Thanksgiving.

The brainwashing continued. Crisco wanted to know why I was so loyal to the United States. He assured me that all I had to do was sign a confession and things would be much improved.

"Do you really think anyone remembers you?" he asked. "Do you really think the Americans care about the prisoners?"

"They care."

"How can you be so sure? Maybe they will sign a peace with my government and go home, leaving all of you here."

"No," I told him. "I remember something from the Korean War that gives me all the faith I need in my government. I remember going out on the battlefield to recover the bodies of my comrades who had been killed. On some such missions we lost additional men. I believe that any government that will go to such trouble to recover its dead will never abandon its living."

"Yes, but even if what you say is true, that is only for the military. You are a civilian."

"A civilian? Why do you say that? I am a lieutenant colonel in the U.S. Army."

"Oh, I am sure you have been given a military rank, but you are not really a soldier. You are CIA."

"I am a career soldier! How can you deny that?" If he was looking for a reaction from me, he got one with this accusation.

"We have information about you," Crisco said. "We know what you are."

I have to confess that Crisco's insistence that I was CIA gave me cause for a lot of worry. I kept trying to push the negative thoughts aside, but it was hard not to dwell on them: Why does this keep coming up? What if they really do believe I'm CIA? I had no idea why such a conviction had been put into their minds, but if they really did believe it, it would mean a great deal of trouble for me. It might be that they wouldn't even let me out when the war was over—as they kept threatening.

Crisco was becoming very upset with my steadfast refusal to agree with him regarding my status. He said, "We, the Vietnamese people, have laws and courts to enforce those laws. You are a criminal of war and you will be tried for your crimes against the Vietnamese people. Your punishment may be ten years to life in prison or even death. However, if you will only refirm your thinking"—I had learned that "refirm my thinking" meant I should agree with their view of the war—"then your conditions will improve. You will be placed in a cell with other Americans, you will be permitted to write to your wife, and when the war is over you will be allowed to go home. If you do not refirm your thinking you will be punished. Now return to your cell and think about your crimes. When you come back here this afternoon, you must be ready to confess your crimes and ask for leniency . . . or face the possibility that you may never go home."

I was very apprehensive when I returned to my cell— probably more frightened than I had been at any time since we were made to face the wall shortly after our capture. My entire life could hang in the balance, tipped one way or the other by whatever was going to happen during the next couple of hours. I felt sick inside. I prayed for guidance and for the courage to endure any outcome.

I heard the turnkey open the door to take me back to the afternoon session. This was it!

Although I had never consciously committed it to memory, the words of the Twenty-third Psalm came to me as I walked with the guard on the way to see Crisco.

> The Lord is my shepherd: I shall not want: He maketh me to lie down in green pastures: He leadeth me beside the still waters. He restoreth my soul: He leadeth me in the paths of righteousness for his name's sake. Yea, though I walk through the valley of the shadow of death, I will fear no evil: for thou art with me: thy rod and thy staff they comfort me. Thou preparest a table before me in the presence of mine enemies: thou anointest my head with oil: my cup runneth over. Surely goodness and mercy shall follow me all the days of my life: and I will dwell in the house of the Lord forever.

Like countless millions before me I found comfort from that most-loved of all Psalms. After that a peace came over

me—a peace that, as the Good Book says, passes all understanding. I knew that I would have periods of depression
again, and I knew that there would be times when the depression would be so acute that it would be all I could do to stand
it. But now, at least, I knew that I had the confidence to deal
with it.

The afternoon session with Crisco began without any for-
mality or the usual polite remarks. He was still steaming with
anger from my comments before the noon meal, and he was
not about to try to be pleasant.

"You've had enough time to think about your crimes,"
he said. "So you tell me now, what is your answer?"

"What I said this morning made you angry, and I do not
want to make you angry again. I have not changed my views
on the war or my status, so I will simply make no further
comments," I replied.

Crisco was holding a pencil in his hand and he snapped
it in two. He was visibly shaken and I could tell that he was
having trouble deciding how to respond to this stubborn
American. After several awkward moments his attitude al-
tered. He smiled slightly and said, "But, don't you understand how much better conditions could be for you?"

"My mind is made up," I replied. "I no longer have any
fear or anxiety for my welfare. I know who holds the keys to
my release from this prison, and it isn't you."

The session ended very abruptly. Crisco sent me back to
my cell with a strong warning.

"We have laws, and we have courts. You will be tried
and punished if you do not refirm your thinking," he said
coldly.

In a way the cold, quiet tone of his prediction was more
frightening than the screaming anger. As I returned to my cell
I didn't know what the future held for me . . . but I knew
who held it. And because of that I was comforted.

9

SPRING RETURNS

We were ready for the move from Boonville in mid-June. It took two long, hard days for the movers to get us packed. I wondered how we had accumulated so much and where we would put it in our smaller Georgia house.

Captain Al Shauf, who was my second FSAO (Family Survivors' Assistance Officer) coordinated the move for us. He did a splendid job, and there weren't even any "suddenly remembered" jobs at the office to take him away from the house when the movers were there. (I wonder if other military wives know what I mean?)

Leaving dear friends behind wasn't easy. The last sight I saw on Pendleton Avenue was our special neighbors, Kyle, Helen, and Audrey Boyer, waving as our car rolled down the street and over the hill heading for Columbus. There were many tears, but I knew this was what we had to do. On the way to Columbus we stopped to tour Helen Keller's homeplace in Alabama. I thought the visit would be of interest to the older children, and it helped break up our trip. Her victory over her own trials and tribulations was an inspiration to me.

The trip was completed without trouble, although we did get lost in Birmingham, where there were several detours due to road construction and not enough road signs to guide a stranger through town. Ben would have been surprised and, I hoped, proud that I could be both driver and navigator.

The previous tenants in our house had received military orders transferring them to another location, so they were gone by May. I have to confess that I would have been glad to see them leave even if we weren't going to move into the house. Twice since Ben was captured their rent checks had bounced, and I really didn't want another problem to handle.

We arrived in Columbus safe and sound, and eager to see our house. Bob and Erma Whitt and their sons Randy and Jimmy had cleaned and repainted the inside of the house despite Bob's recent heart surgery. They were very good friends and super neighbors.

Now I found a new problem. After all the space we had had in our house back in Missouri, we found this house extremely small. It was adequate back in 1955 when Ben and I had only two children, but now there were five. I think this was pointed out to me most graphically when I was walking down the hall past the bathroom and happened to catch a glimpse of the two youngest girls sharing the commode!

We certainly needed a second bathroom, but I didn't see a good way to install one. I kept telling myself hopefully that we wouldn't have to remain in that house for too many months before Ben came home. Until that time we would just have to make do.

After moving in and unpacking a few of the boxes that were necessary to set up housekeeping, I left the other boxes packed and put them in a metal storage shed. David and I spent many hours and lots of sweat putting that shed together. I think the hard work was therapeutic for both of us, and I felt that it drew us together as nothing else had.

An incident that happened between David and me back in Boonville illustrates what a difficult time he was having with the situation. It had to do with the "countdown" calendar by the table in the kitchen and our evening ritual of marking off one more day until Ben returned. Some time after we heard of Ben's status I took the calendar down. This really hurt David, for in his mind it meant I had given up. As long as the calendar was on the wall and we marked off a day at a time, David had faith his dad would come home. But removal of the calendar seemed to be a final act that meant Dad was not coming home soon, and maybe never. Keeping the calendar up was David's way of denying what he didn't want to accept—that his father was missing in action and wasn't coming home on the date we had been counting down to.

After all the work of moving in was taken care of, we took off for the mountains of North Georgia to visit our families. One night while I was visiting Ben's mother, I had a very strange dream. In my dream I was praying, and I asked God when I would know about Ben. Before me on a wall appeared a piece of paper with the number 47. I wondered what the 47 meant . . . was it days, months, years, or what?

After we returned to Columbus I called Ola Smith. We had been friends with Ola and her husband Charles ever since we had been stationed together in Columbus from 1957 to 1959. Like us, Ola and Charles had been members of the Southside Baptist Church. Now, like me, Ola was waiting in Columbus while her husband Charles was serving in Vietnam. The only difference between us was that Charles wasn't a prisoner of war.

"Anne," Ola said when I called. "I'm so glad you called. I've been asking God to send me someone I could help."

After that, Ola often came over to our house after work just to visit. She was a patient listener as I talked about my fears and frustrations. I had never realized before how important a good listener is to someone who is hurting.

Once again our family became active in the Southside Baptist Church. Many of the people who were members there with us in the fifties were still there, so it was a little like coming home. Often on Wednesday night during the prayer service, Bob Whitt included a prayer that Ben's guards would be good to him. That always brought a tear to my eye. The church members were a great support group, just as our friends had been at the church in Boonville.

Margaret Thomas, director of a preschool, asked me if I would teach a class for three-year-old children. The teacher who was supposed to teach that class was moving away because her husband, who was in the army, had received his orders.

I told Margaret I really didn't have to work since Ben's pay and allowances were continuing, despite his MIA status. In that I was very fortunate; the army's policy of pay for the MIA's next of kin had changed since the time of the Korean conflict, when the family of the MIA didn't receive any pay at all.

I also told Margaret that if I did work I felt I needed to work with adults, not children, since I had so many children at home.

"Pray about it, Anne," Margaret said.

I didn't want to pray about it. I was afraid God would want me to do this job and I really didn't want to do it. But I prayed anyway, and as I was afraid he would do, he led me to accept the job.

As it turned out the job was very good for me. There's no way a person can work with eighteen three-year-olds and still feel sorry for herself. I did not have time to be self-centered anymore. I would have never asked for such a job, but it really did help me be a part of life again.

Since Joy was nearly three and our other children were in school, she came to my preschool class, and it was difficult for her. She wanted my undivided attention and had to sit in the corner when she didn't accept the fact that as teacher I had to share my time with all the children in the class. This job became a great learning experience for both Joy and me.

Most of the children in my class had dads in Vietnam. I was always afraid that something bad might happen to one of them. I was so thankful that none of the dads were wounded, killed, or captured. I think it would have been difficult for me to handle the situation if one of them had been hurt.

Christmas was approaching and although I bought gifts and decorated the tree, my heart wasn't in it. In fact, I found myself dreading the season. I couldn't help but wonder if Ben was alive and if he knew it was Christmas. Then the Christmas cards began to arrive, each with a message of concern and telling of prayers for Ben, the children, and me. As a result I managed to find some enjoyment that Christmas Day yet continued to wonder if Ben had even one second of Christmas joy.

I imagined the horrible conditions under which Ben must have been forced to live *if* he had survived these months since the crash. I tried not to dwell on these thoughts, for the tears came easily and far too readily. Often in private I would cry until I had no tears left. Once, however, I cried in front of the children and it so upset them that I tried never to cry in front of them again. They were extremely sensitive to my emotions. What made me sad made them sad. What made me happy made them happy. As the months and years passed I tried to be aware of their fears and not add to them with my tears.

After several months of fears, frustrations, and anxieties, I finally went to God with a very simple prayer. The prayer came from the innermost depths of my heart.

"God, I don't know if Ben is dead or alive, but you do. I don't know where he is, but you do. I love him and I want him to come home to us, but I know you love him even more than I do. I give him to you and I will accept this situation, however you want it to turn out."

In the stillness of that evening my frustrations left me, and for the first time since receiving news of Ben's crash, the path ahead of me appeared clear. Now I had that solid rock upon which to put my dangling feet.

I have since learned that there is a title for this type of prayer. It is called a "prayer of relinquishment." It is a prayer in which you accept that there is nothing you can do except leave the situation in God's hands. Much later, when I learned of Ben's experience with the Twenty-third Psalm and put it together with my prayer of relinquishment, I discovered that we had both been given the gift of serenity at about the same time.

From the time of Ben's crash I had failed to notice my surroundings. I didn't even realize I hadn't seen the seasons change until I noticed the beautiful spring of 1969. I began to wonder why it looked especially lovely to me. Then, as I thought back to the previous spring, I realized my mind had been so focused on Ben and the problems I faced that I had missed it completely. I had let not only spring but many sunrises pass me by.

Now I wanted to face life again, to see the sun come up in the morning instead of dreading the night's end. I wanted to see the rain fall and the flowers bloom. I wanted to live each day, one day at a time, with faith, hope, and gratitude for the things I did have.

Once I had said, "I wish I did not have the responsibility of the children," but now I realized they were my greatest blessing. At last I understood why we were directed to Columbus. It was *my* job, *my* responsibility to take care of our family, pray for Ben, wait for him, and slowly build back our crumbled life brick by brick. That, with God's help, I was trying to do. I just wished there was more I could do to help the POWs.

10

THE DEPRESSION OF

1968

BEN'S STORY

On New Year's Day, 1969, I was looking forward to a
better year than the one just passed. I certainly didn't see any
way it could be worse. I had been a prisoner for close to a
year and in solitary for all but the first two months. I had
received no mail from Anne or from my mom and no news
at all about what was going on in the world. In fact, I didn't
even know where I was imprisoned, although I suspected it
couldn't be too far from a city. I frequently heard trains
nearby and civilian planes in the distance. Could it be Lang
Son? I wanted to know for sure in order to plan an escape.

In the summer and fall I had been terribly depressed,
although I seemed to have passed through the worst period
and was now doing somewhat better. The improved diet at
K–77 had slowed down my weight loss, and I had started a
mild exercise program, mainly just pacing back and forth in
my cell and doing a few sit-ups and push-ups on my cot. Even

so, during those exercise periods my mind managed to forget for a few moments that I was depressed, and I felt better all over. I came to realize that I simply must keep my mind and body active if I expected to survive this ordeal.

In September I had remembered Sherri's birthday and thought of all the gifts I'd give her if only I could. She needed a new tricycle when I left for Vietnam but may have reached the age that she preferred a small bicycle with training wheels. Whatever she needed, I was confident that Anne had made the day a very special one for her.

The months of October, November, and December had contained several occasions that made me homesick and very sad. Mom's birthday on October 11, David's on October 27, Cliff's on November 9, and Joy's on December 11 had brought back many memories of happier days. I thought of my family constantly, but particularly on their birthdays.

November 21 had been especially hard for me. That was the ninth anniversary of the death of Clarice. All day long I could do nothing but think about her lovely face and her soft voice. I could almost feel her tender arms around my neck that night in the hospital as I kissed her good-bye for the last time. My only moment of peace that entire day came when I recalled Christ's promise that we would meet again.

Thanksgiving Day had gone practically unnoticed—no turkey or dressing, but stewed pumpkin soup for the umpteenth time. The greatest feeling of loss, of course, was the absence of our family circle.

For lunch on Christmas Day I had been taken into an interrogation room, where Crisco and the camp commander were seated behind a table. The commander had indicated for me to sit down on the stool nearby and then started speaking as Crisco interpreted.

"You are a criminal of war . . . your country is the aggressor in South Vietnam. If you had not come to Vietnam to kill our people, you would be at home with your family enjoying Christmas Day."

I had felt lonely enough without having to listen to this harangue, but he kept on.

"Because the Vietnamese people are concerned for your

welfare, we have shown you every lenient treatment and have prepared for you a good meal. Enjoy your meal as you think about your crimes and your family."

The commander and Crisco had departed and a trustee had put before me a plate of food. It contained one-half of a turkey leg, a small serving of sweet and sour pork, and a loaf of French bread. At this moment I was torn between two strong emotions: my starving body cried out for food, but my mind did not want to give the old goat the satisfaction of winning a psychological battle. I deeply resented the camp commander's hypocritical actions.

My hungry body won the battle. But I was still determined that I would win the war.

Then late on New Year's Eve I heard the turnkey unlocking my cell. It was the first time he had done so during the night, and I wondered what was up.

Crisco was with the guard. He handed me a small plate of cookies and a bottle of beer. I was shocked when Crisco said, "This is for your New Year's celebration."

I am a teetotaler and had not drunk so much as a beer since the one cold can of beer I drank in Korea in 1951. I drank this one, though. It was a welcome change from hot water.

On January 9, 1969, I learned that peace talks between the U.S. and Vietnam would begin in Paris very soon. The cadre who told me the news also added that "the war must end by January 20, 1969." His rationale was that since this was an illegal war, at least in Vietnam's view, Johnson would be obligated to end the conflict before he left office on the twentieth.

I believed him when he said the peace talks were about to begin. I had to believe him in order to rekindle my hopes for freedom. I didn't agree with his optimistic view that the war would end so quickly. Still I wished with all my heart that he was right.

The following days and weeks passed quickly. I began to think that the war would soon be over and started making plans for my return to America. Also, with the talk of peace the food got better, and we began receiving a piece of warm French bread, a spoonful of sugar, and a cup of hot water for breakfast each day except Sunday. I wondered if the Vietnamese really thought this belated act of kindness would sweeten the prisoners' memories of the many months of near-starvation diets. Surely, I thought, they couldn't be so naive.

Another noticeable improvement was the receipt of mimeographed pages of news. The camp officials prepared a typed copy of the daily Hanoi Radio propaganda broadcasts and circulated them within the prison.

I began to use these newsletters as a means of communication with other prisoners. As I read the news, I would underline various letters using a split piece of bamboo as a pen and ink made from soot and water. The soot was obtained by placing my metal drinking cup very close to the flame of the kerosene lamp that burned in my cell all night—not for warmth but so that the guards could see what I was doing. I hoped that other Americans would notice the messages concealed in the series of underlined letters and send a few my way. To my great disappointment I never received any evidence that other prisoners noticed the signals.

Another improvement was that I was provided books to read. Reading really helped the time pass more swiftly and was educational as well.

Once I was given the complete works of Shakespeare, which brought me tremendous pleasure. I pored over the words of his plays and found meaning and excitement I never knew was there. I would have given anything in the world to see Professor Ray's face as I devoured these books. Professor Ray was my tenth-grade English teacher, and I was his poorest student.

"Ben, have you learned your soliloquy from *Macbeth*?"

"No, sir."

"And why not?"

"It just doesn't make sense to me, Professor Ray. 'Tomorrow, and tomorrow, and tomorrow, creeps in this petty pace from day to day.' What does that mean?"

I knew what it meant now, as all the tomorrows crept at a snail's pace from day to day in K-77. I knew exactly what it meant.

Professor Ray would never expect to hear this from me, but that Shakespeare guy could really write.

Another book I was given to read was entitled *How the Steel Was Tempered*. It was written by a young Russian revolutionary named Nikolai Obstrosky. One of his statements struck me as particularly meaningful.

Man's most precious possession is life. It is given to him but once and he ought to live it so as to have no torturous regrets of wasted years. To never know the burning shame of a mean and petty past. So live that dying he might say, "All my life, all my strength I've given for the greatest cause in all the world . . . the struggle for the liberation of mankind."

I realized that that struggle was still going on in the world. It was a struggle for peace, for freedom, and for the dignity of mankind. I saw myself as having been a real part of that struggle, both in Korea in 1951 and 1952 and again in Vietnam as we tried to help the citizens of South Vietnam obtain true freedom and democracy. A soldier must believe his cause is just and honorable or else he would be nothing more than a mercenary. I believed strongly in the causes I had served!

We now had a radio too, if one wanted to call it that. There was a loudspeaker in the compound that played for an hour each Sunday. Sometimes we would hear news. The news generally consisted of telling us how many victories the freedom fighters of South Vietnam were winning against the American aggressors, along with the latest report on how many schools, orphanages, hospitals, and churches our criminal pilots had bombed in the last twenty-four hours. To hear the Vietnamese tell it, we never managed to hit a target that didn't fall under one of those categories.

The Vietnamese didn't realize it, but the prisoners learned to judge the effectiveness of the bombing raids according to the reports. A school was a light raid; a school and a church meant a medium raid; and a school, a church, and a hospital indicated a heavy and effective raid.

When they weren't playing their brand of news for us, we listened to talk of enlightenment from a propaganda official telling us to confess our crimes and beg the forgiveness of the Vietnamese people. Sometimes, I am sorry to say, we also heard the taped confessions of other American prisoners of war who had been coerced into saying things they really didn't believe. Whenever I heard one of those tapes, I was more than ever convinced that I would never let them break my will.

On the twentieth of January, 1969, I spent many hours thinking about Anne and our life together. It was our eighteenth anniversary, and to celebrate the event I decided to make a replacement for the wedding ring that Armband had taken from me on the day I was captured. I did this by heating the handle of my toothbrush over the kerosene lamp until it was pliable. Then I bent it around my finger and broke it. There was no mistaking it for the gold wedding band Anne had given me, but it felt good to have a memento of our love on my finger again.

II

INFORMATION HAS
BEEN RECEIVED . . .

ANNE'S STORY

On the first day of spring, 1969, my FSAO, Captain Oscar E. Knight, called and asked if he could come out to the house. When he arrived he handed me a piece of paper which read:

Info has been received which reveals that your husband survived the aircraft crash on 8 Feb 68, and was taken prisoner by the enemy. This info was recently obtained through intelligence sources but we have not been able to determine the date of the information pertaining to your husband. There was no information concerning his physical condition or whether he was injured in the crash. The information did indicate one of the other five individuals aboard the helicopter was killed as a result of the crash. Based upon the receipt of this information, DA is officially changing his status from missing to captured.

   Additional information concerning this change will
be provided by letter from the ADJ GEN, Department
of the Army.

   For my own self-preservation I had, after thirteen
months as an MIA wife, faced each side. Ben might come
home; he might not. I had not given up hope that he
would return, but on the other hand I had never felt entirely confident that he would. I suppose one could call my
position at this time as "middle of the road." I had also
shared these feelings with our children so that they too
could face the fact that Ben might not return. In this way
I hoped they would be as prepared for the eventuality as
much as one can possibly be prepared. Therefore, this
news, which arrived on the first day of spring, did not
change my attitude very much.
   The one thing it did change was that I was now allowed
to write a letter to Ben twice a month and send a package
every other month. They could be mailed free through the
postal system. The prospect of sending letters and packages
to Ben was exciting, and I eagerly looked forward to doing
so, hoping he would receive them.
   In the packages I included maple-nut candy, Dentyne
chewing gum, butterscotch Life Savers, reading and writing
materials, and even some over-the-counter medical supplies.
I also stuffed the empty spaces with photographs of the latest
clothing styles and automobiles as well as catalogs showing
the newest consumer items. Once I included tweezers for Ben
to use on the eyelashes that kept growing into his eye following minor surgery some years before. I felt certain the packages would be opened for inspection and some items held
back, but maybe a few would eventually reach him. I knew
that if he received the candy, gum, or tweezers he would put
two and two together and know they were from me . . . anything to let him know we were aware of his situation and that
we cared.
   Getting the items together to send to Ben was an adven-
ture, and I imagined how receipt of them would bring him
some happiness. But North Vietnam refused to accept the

packages, and as each one was returned I began to lose my enthusiasm for putting them together. I felt there was no use in doing so.

Then just before Christmas 1969 the Department of the Army informed me that an extra-large package could be mailed. I decided to try one more time. This package was not returned, and I continued sending others, which also were never returned. My hopes were high. Maybe Ben was getting something from home.

The thrill of being allowed to write soon turned into an emotional drain. First, I was provided an address in Cambodia where I could send a letter with no restrictions on content. Then some few months later I was sent preprinted letter forms prepared by our government at the direction of North Vietnam. The forms had six blank lines printed on a paper along with directions in English and Vietnamese. This was the only way I was permitted to correspond.

I wrote my messages on these brief forms and sent them to Madame Binh, the chief negotiator for the Viet Cong at the Paris peace talks. We were instructed to write, or preferably type, our message on the form and speak only about family and health. Then we were instructed to write a personal letter to Mme. Binh appealing to her to forward the letter to the POW. These two letters were mailed in the same envelope to her Paris address.

I found it extremely difficult to write the personal letter to Mme. Binh. What could I possibly say to convince her to help me? There was so much I wanted to tell Ben, but being limited to just six short lines, I spent hours trying to decide what was most important to write. Out of all this frustration and because I felt that if Mme. Binh would not send a letter through for a wife, perhaps she would for a mother, I asked Ben's mom to write once a month. None of our letters were ever returned, and we held onto a thread of hope that they were getting through to Ben if he was alive.

The peace talks in Paris gave us a measure of hope, but they were going extremely slowly—too slowly for the MIAs and POWs and for us, the families who waited and wondered. Time passed at a snail's pace. The talks could not get under-

way until the shape of the negotiating table could be determined. It took almost a year for North Vietnam to finally
agree to a round table. I wanted Ben home so much that I
couldn't see what difference it made how the table was
shaped. What we were interested in was the shape of our
men! I didn't care whether the negotiators stood up or sat on
the floor. I just wanted them to get on with the important
part of their meeting, adherence to the Geneva Convention,
which required:

1. Release of names of prisoners held
2. Immediate release of sick and wounded prisoners
3. Impartial inspection of prisoner-of-war facilities
4. Proper treatment of all prisoners
5. Regular flow of mail

To me time was of the utmost importance, but to those
in a position to determine the fate of those of us involved,
time seemed insignificant. It was things like this that frustrated me and made me want to run up and down the street
and scream, "Does anybody care?"

Nevertheless, Ben's status change on the first day of
spring was a significant indication to me that there was a
new path to follow, a new beginning. Perhaps I should
have put more faith in the news than I did, but I was
sheltering myself from the terrible pain of not hearing from
Ben. With no real news about him I was in limbo, and
the middle-of-the-road feelings helped me survive. I was
trying to live life one day at a time . . . sometimes even
half a day at a time.

Back in June when I had unpacked the boxes necessary
to set up housekeeping and stored the others, I had stored all
the pictures and knick-knacks that add warmth and personal-
ity to a house. One day Ola Smith came over and told me
she was going to help me get those boxes out of storage and
unpack them.

We worked hard. Midnight came and we were still working. I slowed down, hoping she would take the hint and stop,
but she didn't. That night the boxes were completely unpacked and our home really became cozy and warm for the

first time since we had come to Columbus. It was now a place where we could enjoy living while we waited for Ben. I realized then that I should have done this sooner. I shouldn't have had to wait for Ola to push me into it.

But I was ever grateful that she had asked God to send her someone she could help and that I was the one he chose to send.

12

ESCAPE FROM K-77

BEN'S STORY

During the first fourteen months of my stay in K-77 I was moved from cell 1 to cell 18, then back to cell 1, then in early September 1969, back again to cell 18. I had wanted to escape earlier, but for a long time I didn't even know where I was located in reference to any geographic feature. I knew I was near a large city, maybe Lang Son near the Chinese border, because I continued to hear trains and what sounded like commercial airliners. But Crisco consistently refused to tell me where I was being held. He would only say, "You are on Vietnamese territory."

Then in June of 1969 I obtained some of the critical information I needed so that I could begin to seriously consider an escape. A friendly guard who had told me his name was On' came to my cell during the noon rest period one day and wanted to talk. His gold-crowned tooth shone brightly as he said, "Today I go Hanoi, see movie."

"That's nice," I said, smiling. "Which way is Hanoi?"

He pointed toward the northeast.

"How far?"

Then On' held up ten fingers, and since kilometers was

the standard unit of measurement in Vietnam, I deduced that we were approximately six miles southwest of Hanoi.

This was the first real information I had received as to where I was being detained on Vietnamese territory. It was at that precise moment that I made my decision to attempt an escape—to travel to Hanoi during the hours of darkness, locate the French consulate, and request political asylum.

Many questions had to be answered: How would I get out of my cell? Then the prison? Then North Vietnam? Each obstacle seemed exponentially more difficult than the one before.

Cells 1 and 18 were essentially the same: thick concrete walls coated with plaster and a high vaulted ceiling. There was no window to either cell, but there were bars in the top half of the door and a wooden shutter that covered the bars. The shutter was left open so the prisoners could look out into the courtyard, except at night or whenever there was another prisoner in the yard. The bottom half of the door was made of hard wood over one inch thick.

Wood!

Woodworking was one of my hobbies, and I had worked with all sorts of wood. I had cut it and shaped it and made it do my will. I believed that if I had the tools I could also make this piece of wood do my will.

But what did it accomplish to think such thoughts? They were no different from my fantasy of pole-vaulting over the wall. Anyway, even if I got through the door I would still be in the compound, so what good would it do me?

But, I reasoned, if I got into the compound at the right time, say in the middle of the night when the guards weren't all that alert, I might be able to get over the wall.

So what? I asked myself. Even if I got over the wall I would still be in the middle of North Vietnam. Where would I go from there?

Am I not even going to try? I thought then. The Code of Conduct, which had been so important to me, says that if I am captured I will make every attempt to escape. What attempt had I made?

None.

All right, I thought, then we were back to the door. It

was a heavy wooden door. How could I possibly get through it without the necessary tools? I decided I would make the tools. I had to consider how I was going to do this. There were many imponderables, but I wasn't going to let that stop me from trying. I had now made up my mind to escape and I had every intention of doing it.

I started work. There were several pieces of wire embedded in the plaster walls, put there so we could hang mosquito netting over our cots at night. It was a good stout wire rather like the wire used in American coat hangers. I dug a piece of this wire out of the plaster using a bamboo sliver and then I made a drill by bending the wire around a bamboo handle. The drill worked remarkably well for making holes in the door panel. My best guess was I was going to have to drill about two hundred of them.

Two hundred holes was a lot of work, and it was going to take several days, possibly several weeks, but what else did I have to do?

I drilled holes for over a week. At first the drilling was a slow process, but the speed picked up as I gained experience and confidence. There were a couple of reasons for the improvements. One was that I learned how to use the drill more effectively as time progressed, but the other was my "watch-chicken."

There were chickens clucking and cackling and scratching around the yard all the time, and when the shutter was open I could look through the bars at them. I liked to watch them just to pass the time. There was one rooster I particularly liked to watch. He was the cockiest little thing I had ever seen, strutting around like he owned the whole world.

One day I threw a bread crumb out to him and he came over to my cell door to eat it. He was entertaining to watch, so I got into the habit of throwing out a few crumbs to him after each meal. In return, he developed the habit of hanging around my door to wait for the crumbs. Then one day the little rooster squawked and ran away. A moment later the guard walked by. When the guard was gone the rooster came back. After that happened several times I said to myself, "Ben, what does that tell you?"

Up until that moment, my practice had been to drill for

a few seconds, wait and listen intently, then drill some more. That type of drilling was very time-consuming. After I learned that the rooster would stand watch for me, I was able to work for long periods without fear of being discovered. I was able to speed up my work to about three times faster than it had been going.

Drilling so many holes, however, presented me with two immediate problems. One was what to do with the sawdust that came from the holes. That one was easy to solve. I kept the floor swept clean as a whistle and the sawdust went into the toilet bucket. The toilet bucket was emptied twice a day, by me, so there was never so much residue as to make anyone suspicious.

The next step was to fill in the holes I had already drilled so that they wouldn't be noticed when my cell was inspected. I came up with a pretty good way to handle that problem. I mixed a few bread crumbs and some toothpaste with soot obtained from the kerosene lamp. The result was a type of plastic wood, roughly the same color as the gray door. As soon as I finished a hole I filled it in with the plastic-wood mixture. When the mixture dried the holes were all but invisible.

But the holes weren't enough. I had to cut between the holes, which meant I needed a chisel. For that I found an extra sixpenny nail in my bunk. It took me a couple of days working it back and forth before I was able to get it out, but I finally got it. The next step was to make a chisel out of the nail. I flattened the nail by dragging it back and forth across the concrete floor until the point was flat and sharp like a chisel. Next, I rubbed the nail's head on the floor until it was basically square. This would prevent it from turning inside the handle I was to make for it.

To make the handle I first pressed a layer of bread down around the top of the square nail head, compressing it tightly against the nail with a shoelace. Then I hung the nail by a small wire over the kerosene lamp. Baking the bread all night made it very hard. The next day I pressed down a second layer of bread and baked it all night, and then each day I made another layer until I had a palm-sized handle of bread that had been baked hard as a rock. When I finished, the handle worked perfectly.

I sat on the floor by the door drilling holes and chiseling wood while my little watch-chicken pulled sentry duty for me as surely as if he had stood "guard mount."

"Rooster," I said, speaking so quietly that not even the chicken just outside my door could hear me, "what is the fifth general order?"

I answered for him. "Sir, my fifth general order is to quit my post only when properly relieved."

"Very good," I said, working out another splinter of wood. "See that you remember that. Oh, and maybe you'd better get a haircut before tomorrow morning's inspection."

As I played the silly little game of guard mount with the rooster, I continued to work, and as I worked I planned the next stage of the operation.

I still had the canvas duffle bag they had given me at Bao Cao. I measured the canvas pretty carefully, and I believed I could make a ladder as well as a canvas map case and fatigue cap to use as a disguise. Most Vietnamese officers, I noticed, had a canvas map case.

Of course the canvas strips wouldn't be much wider than a rope, but because there would be places for hand- and foot-holds, it would be a lot easier to climb than a rope. I figured it would take me about an hour to make the ladder, so I decided not to even start on it until I was ready to go. However, the map case and cap would require lots of time to make, so I decided to start on them right away.

Once I got over the wall, I planned to go to Hanoi and turn myself in to the French consulate. There I would ask for asylum, and even if they couldn't send me out of the country on the next courier flight I would at least have a more comfortable stay and, more importantly, would be able to get word through to my government and family. The trick, of course, would be to get to the consulate without being caught. I obviously wouldn't be able to blend in with the people, even though there were a lot of occidentals in Hanoi. But I hoped that if I turned my uniform inside out so that the prison stripes wouldn't show and if I spoke only French, I might get away with it.

It took three months of intense preparation to get everything ready, but on December 7, 1969, I was ready for my escape attempt. I didn't stop to think about it until I was ready to go, but this was Pearl Harbor Day. Our country had suffered a setback that day twenty-eight years before. Maybe I could make up for some of it this night.

I waited until 10:00 P.M. The camp was very quiet and I hadn't heard a guard for a long time. As planned, I turned the prison uniform inside out, donned my cap and map case, and set about making the ladder. Since my watch-chicken had gone away to roost I had to be doubly cautious. The roving guard could be just outside my cell.

The last step in my plan was to rumple up one of my two blankets and spread the second over it. I hoped this ruse would fool the guard as he made his rounds throughout the night, thus giving me a buffer of time before morning wake-up.

I wasn't frightened, but I was very alert and somewhat anxious. I decided that was probably good; a little apprehension would make me more cautious. I prayed a quick little prayer.

"Lord, help me in my time of danger. Fill my heart with the courage to face the unknown one more time. Amen."

After I prayed, I listened carefully to see if I could hear anything or anyone on the other side of the door. When I was certain the coast was clear, I removed the panel. That part of the plan went beautifully. The panel slipped out just as it was designed to.

I had been aware that another American prisoner was being held in a cell close to mine. Just before leaving my cell, I decided to write a note to him and drop it through the bars of his cell door when I got out. Using a bamboo stick for a pen, soot and water as ink, and brown toilet paper, I wrote the following:

My name is Ben Purcell. I am an LTC, U.S. Army. I have succeeded in removing a panel from my cell door and have escaped. If I don't make it home by the time the war is over please contact my wife and tell her I tried. She is Anne Purcell and she lives on Pendleton Avenue in Boonville, Missouri. Thanks and God bless you.

The next step after removing the panel was to crawl through the door. I took a deep breath and then poked my head and shoulders through. That was probably my most anxious moment, for there was a great deal of potential danger. If there had been a guard standing near my door he would have been justified in shooting me or thrusting a bayonet into my body. I also worried about my little watch-chicken. I knew he was asleep, but what if he heard something and decided to crow about it? It would be a terrible case of irony if my little rooster turned on me now.

Scarcely daring to breathe, I crawled out through the hole; then I put the panel back in place so that the guard wouldn't notice anything wrong as he made his next inspection tour and wouldn't realize I was gone until the morning check when all prisoners were let out, one at a time, to empty their toilet buckets.

Clutching the canvas ladder and map case, I moved as quietly as I could around the cell block and into the administrative portion of the prison. At one time I passed through an archway and heard a person snoring less than three feet from me. I thought it would be a terrible stroke of bad luck at that moment to step on a dog's tail.

I continued on to the perimeter fence around the administrative area, where it was only about eight feet high. I threw the ladder up and over a rock embedded in the top of the wall and climbed up, dodging the broken glass also embedded on top as well as the electric wires strung just above the wall. It was so easy that I almost let out a shout of joy! I could not see the ground outside the wall but took a blind jump and landed upright without sprained ankles or broken bones.

Once outside the prison compound I walked as quickly as possible to get away from the vicinity of the prison. Now I had to put the next part of my plan into operation, and that meant finding Hanoi.

I knew there was a railroad track nearby because I had heard the trains from my cell. The track would lead me by the most direct and level route to the center of Hanoi, perhaps even passing close to the French consulate.

I started in the direction where, based on the sounds I

Here we are back in March of 1950. This was the day I graduated from North Georgia College and was commissioned as Second Lieutenant, Regular Army. Anne was finishing her freshman year at North Georgia.

This is Clarice Anne, our first daughter, before she became ill with rheumatoid arthritis.

Our wedding day. At five P.M. on January 20, 1951, Anne and I were married in the small Baptist church in Baldwin, Georgia. (Cameron Studio—Cornelia, GA)

This is the last family picture before I left for Vietnam in August of 1967. (top) Anne, Joy, and myself. (bottom) Debbie, Sherri, Clifford, and David. Little did we know that our next reunion would be five-and-a-half years later. (Toenes Studio—Boonville, MO)

Ben always liked to do carpentry work for relaxation and in Vietnam he helped build the berms around his office. This was a typical photograph of "our Ben" and we kept it on the refrigerator until he returned in March 1973.

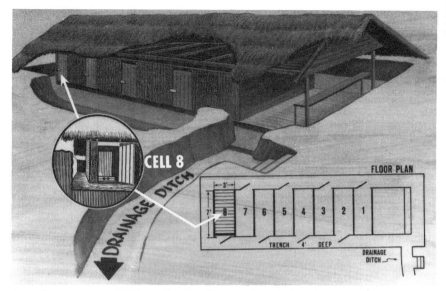

An artist's concept of "Camp Bao Cao" somewhere in North Vietnam. When I was placed in solitary in a small cell here in early 1968 I could never have guessed that it would be almost 58 months before I would be permitted to speak with another American. (U.S. Army War College)

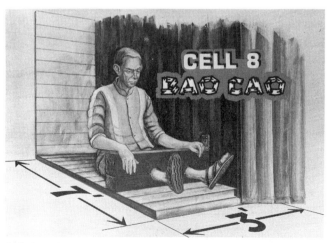

This is a sketch of cell #8 at "Bao Cao" showing the stocks which were used to punish prisoners who did not cooperate during the interrogation process or who refused to "refirm their thinking" during the brainwash sessions. (U.S. Army War College)

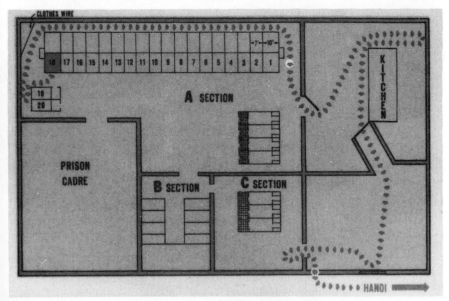

After removing a panel from the bottom half of the door and slipping out of my cell late on December 7, 1969, I evaded the roving prison guard by taking this route through the prison compound. (U.S. Army War College)

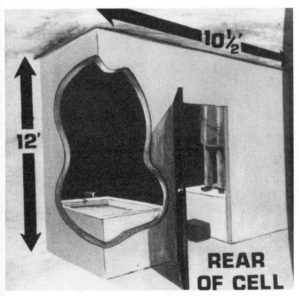

At a camp I dubbed "K-49," Charlie, the working dummy, served as a ruse to deceive the guards during my second escape on March 18, 1972. (U.S. Army War College)

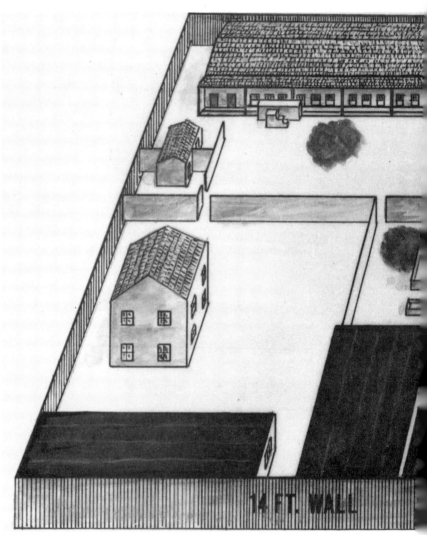

14 FT. WALL

"K-77" was a maximum security prison located about six miles southwest of Hanoi. I was detained here from July 8, 1968 until mid-December, 1971. (U.S. Army War College)

8 FT WALL

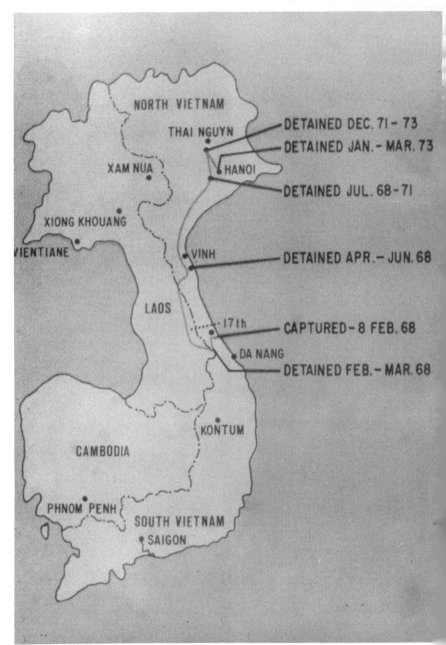

My captors took us along one of the many Ho Chi Minh trails from our point of capture in Eastern Laos to North Vietnam where we were held for more than five years in three different prison camps. (U.S. Army War College)

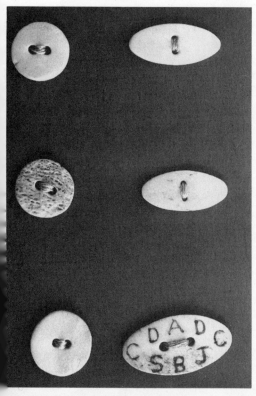

The only way I remained sane during those many years of solitary confinement was to work with my hands. After my two escapes, when it became too dangerous to plan more breakouts, I took to craftsmanship. Here is a communion set I made out of aluminum from empty toothpaste tubes and also a set of buttons made from bones found in my soup. On the button in the lower right corner, I carved the first initial of each member of my family. (Rudeseal and Associates)

When I received word that Ben was missing-in-action my first thought was "Oh, if only I didn't have the children." However, in the years that followed I discovered they were my greatest blessing. (U.S. Army, Fort Benning)

Our Debbie and Clifford were very anxious to do their part for their Dad and the other POWs. Here they mail letters to the North Vietnamese delegation in Paris demanding adherence to the Geneva Convention tenets concerning POWs. (U.S. Army, Fort Benning)

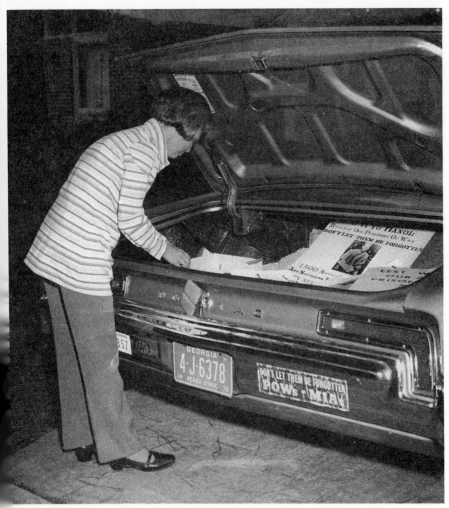

I was co-chairman of the National League of Families in Columbus, Georgia. This is my mobile office for the projects I worked on to provide humane treatment for American POWs in Vietnam. (U.S. Army, Fort Benning)

Periodically our National League chapter in Columbus, Georgia, sent petitions and letters to the Paris Peace Talks. We never wanted the North Vietnamese or the Viet Cong to think we had forgotten our men. Here, David and Sherri are helping with a mailing project. (U.S. Army, Fort Benning)

Here I am reporting to Air Force General Ogan at the Hanoi Airport on my release on March 27, 1973. Each of the 1874 days I spent in prison brought a fresh hope for freedom and each night I went to bed disappointed. On the 1875th day my hope was realized. (U.S. Army)

Here we are after watching Ben's arrival in the Philippines—at last he was on friendly soil. For five-and-a-half years we had read from the Bible and prayed for his safe return—this gave us the strength to hope and the determination to live each day as it came. (*Ledger-Inquirer,* Columbus, GA)

This was one of the most poignant moments of my homecoming—David, a cadet at West Point, class of '75, said he didn't know whether to salute or hug me first. His salute had to be the most meaningful one of my military career—then he gave me a big hug. (*Ledger-Inquirer,* Columbus, GA)

At Clark Air Base we were given physical examinations, debriefed, and fed delicious meals. Then, 32 free and happy American ex-POWs posed for a photograph. (USAF, Clark AFB)

This family photograph, made for the Army War College directory class of 1974, showed me how much the children had grown in the five-and-a-half years Ben was away. (U.S. Army War College)

One of the many welcome-home ceremonies for me was at Fort Benning, Georgia. (U.S. Army, Fort Benning)

had heard, I thought the track was. But after I went about a mile without finding it, I feared I was going in the wrong direction.

I backtracked, passed the prison, and went off in the opposite direction hoping to find the tracks. Again I was unsuccessful. I came back by the prison a second time and went off in yet another direction. Again I was unsuccessful. I passed the prison yet again but still couldn't find the cotton-picking railroad track!

It was a very dark and misty night, even darker than normal because the Vietnamese were so frightened of our air attacks that they maintained blackout conditions all the time. There were no stars to give me a bearing. Also, I had never really seen any of the area around the prison, so I had no idea of direction. I was as lost as if I had been wandering around in the middle of the Sahara Desert. I can't begin to describe the level of frustration I felt then. I had spent weeks and weeks preparing for my escape, and once successfully out of the prison I found that I was unable to do a simple thing like find the nearest train out of town. The first major glitch of my escape had occurred, and it was already growing light. I could easily have made the six miles to Hanoi during the night, and I had hoped to find the French consulate during the hours of darkness.

Now that was no longer possible.

I hid in a ditch alongside the road for a while and wondered what would be the best thing to do. Finally, I figured that it might be less suspicious if I just walked along the road as if I had every right to do so.

I climbed up out of the ditch, brushed my hands off, and started walking in the direction that I hoped was Hanoi. I met four or five people but none of them gave me a second look. My plan seemed to be working. Gradually the gloom and despair began fading away. I was going to make it . . . I was actually putting it over on them!

A man came by on a bicycle and then stopped and looked back at me. I knew he was puzzled as to who this European was who was walking down the road so early in the morning. He asked me something in Vietnamese and I replied, in poor French, "Could you direct me to the French consulate, please?"

"*Oui,*" he answered. He patted the carrier on the back of his bike, offering me a ride. I thanked him and climbed on.

He said nothing; he just pedaled quietly as we zipped along toward Hanoi. We passed several men, women, and schoolchildren walking to work or school. None of them seemed in the least surprised to see an occidental perched on the back of a bicycle.

As I watched the people moving about in their early-morning activities, I couldn't help but compare them with the people I had seen elsewhere. And I thought they were really no different. They were families; they worried about going to work, about their kids' making good grades in school, about what to wear, about what to cook for supper.

I wondered why we were no better able to avoid war and thought that maybe if President Nixon could be in my place, riding on the back of a bicycle in the morning rush-hour in Hanoi, he could understand how I felt. Then I smiled at the thought. I believed I had hit upon a new method of achieving world peace. Put the president of the United States on the back of a bicycle in Hanoi early in the morning. Put Ho Chi Minh in the front seat of a pickup truck in Clarkesville, Georgia, on a Saturday afternoon. Then the world leaders would understand what the rest of us already know.

My daydream ended as we came to the outskirts of Hanoi. By now there were hundreds of bicycles and thousands of people milling about, and still no one seemed to be paying any particular attention to me. We rode next to trolleys, zipped along with other bicycles, and moved in and out of a stream of military truck traffic. Finally we arrived at a small building with an open front much like a booth at a carnival.

My good fortune had just run out, for we had stopped in front of a police precinct station. I saw several policemen. The rider spoke to a couple of them and they started toward us. I groaned. Either my ride had known from the beginning that I was an American prisoner of war or he didn't know where the Embassy was and was asking for directions. In either case I knew I was a goner.

I decided to play my hand as strongly as I could, however, so when I got off the bike I thanked my friend for the ride. I smiled and bowed at him and he returned my smile and bowed back. Then, happily, he pedaled on his way.

The police spoke to me in Vietnamese and I answered in French, asking to be taken to the French consulate. They took me into the police station instead.

I stayed in a small room in the police station for a couple of hours. As I waited they served me a cup of tea and a piece of French bread with some sugar on it, similar to the food I had been getting at the prison for breakfast. Several times they came in to speak to me, and every time I asked to be taken to the French consulate. Then I heard someone in the outer office speaking French. Not Vietnamese French but French French. Before long three men entered the room where I sat behind a small table. Two were obviously Vietnamese, but the third man appeared to be a Frenchman. He wore a French beret and leather shoes and carried a leather briefcase. One of the two Vietnamese spoke fluent French, the other rather good English. First the French-speaking interrogator asked me a few complicated questions. Although I had studied French in college and had served in France for three years, my knowledge of the language was insufficient for me to answer properly. Then the second interrogator asked, "Do you speak English?"

"Yes."

"Are you a pilot?"

"No. I am an American serviceman, but I was captured in South Vietnam, and your soldiers brought me to North Vietnam." It was obvious to me by this time that the policeman would not let the Frenchman talk to me, so I decided to respond to the Vietnamese interrogators' questions in a loud voice hoping that the French official could understand English.

"I am Lieutenant Colonel Ben Purcell. I am an American prisoner of war. I have been detained in solitary confinement for more than a year and have not been permitted to write to my family."

The French official's face registered some interest but I still didn't know whether he understood me or not. How utterly frustrating the situation had become. After I responded to a few more questions from the Vietnamese interpreter the Frenchman left, and at that moment I was crushed.

Within an hour Crisco, the camp commander, two guards, and a driver appeared at the police station to take me back to K-77. I wasn't returned to cell 18 but was taken to cell 2, the punishment cell.

I was told to lie down on the wooden boards which served as a bed and had stocks. It was an uncomfortable position and the stocks hurt my ankles, but I was not depressed. In fact, I would almost say my mood was buoyant.

I believe the thing that most lifted my spirits was the fact that I had tried to escape. I didn't make it all the way home, but I did try. And with a few breaks I could have made it. My spirits were also lifted, even in this period of disappointment, as I gazed at the small cross on the wall that I had fashioned from two slender bones taken from my soup.

I noticed something else, too. Although Crisco and Spit were as harsh as ever, the guards were treating me with a noticeable increase of respect. It reminded me of the feeling I had when we stopped at the field hospital on the trail north. It was as if although we were soldiers from enemy countries, we were still brothers in arms and we shared the common bond of duty and honor. They may not have respected many of the things that were dear to me, such as democracy, freedom, or the flag, but they did respect honor. They realized that it was an honorable thing for a prisoner of war to try to escape.

There was another benefit to my escape. For the first time since my capture I felt alive! While I was planning and working on my escape, the hours were consumed and the days didn't seem to drag as badly. So even though I had been placed in stocks as punishment, I had regained much of my self-respect. That was vitally important to me because it had all but vanished when I surrendered after the helicopter crash in February of 1968.

I was alive and well. I was glad I had done it, and I vowed that if another opportunity ever presented itself I would do it again.

I had had very few privileges before I made my escape so I figured I had nothing to lose. One privilege I did have that I hadn't thought about was the freedom to move around.

Now I could no longer look through the bars at the courtyard or just pace up and down in my cell. (At Bao Cao I couldn't pace back and forth in the three-by-seven-foot cell, but I could in this one, and the exercise was good for me.) For two weeks after my escape they kept me in leg stocks.

Crisco had a hard time getting over my escape attempt. He told me again and again that I had done a bad thing and that I had made trouble for him by escaping. I think he took it personally.

One morning Spit came into my cell, unlocked the stocks, and took me outside for an interview with Crisco.

Crisco had his back to me when I arrived and stood that way for a long time, as if to show me that he was in charge. He ran his hand through his very black, bushy hair a few times and then finally turned and looked at me. He shook his head as if he were very disappointed with me.

"We have treated you well, but you do this," he said.

"You have not treated me well."

"How can you say that? I let you keep the cross you made even after you escaped," he said. "And you are fed well."

"We might discuss the food sometime."

His eyes narrowed. "You are given the same food we give our soldiers. Do you think you should be fed better than our army? What would our people think if they knew we were feeding the enemy criminals better than we feed our own soldiers?"

"All right, let's say the food is okay," I replied. "Why have you kept me in isolation all this time? I know you have other American prisoners here. Why do you not let me see them? Why can't I talk to them?"

Crisco folded his arms across his chest as if he were a stern schoolmaster chastising a young pupil.

"You have done nothing to recant your crimes against the Vietnamese people. You have made no statements; you have signed no confessions. When you do this, I will know your attitude has changed. Then, and only then, will you be able to talk to your fellow countrymen."

"I won't do that."

"Why did you try to escape?"

"I'm a soldier. It is a soldier's duty to escape."

"Do you think the people in your country would honor

you if you escaped? You have been in prison for a long time, so you don't know what it's like in America now. In America the people are burning flags and marching in the streets to demand that this unjust war be stopped."

"I don't believe it."

"You have heard the news on our broadcasts," Crisco said.

"Propaganda."

"No, not propaganda," Crisco said. "Some of your most famous people . . . a very famous actress has said that the war is wrong."

"Well, that's what makes America great," I replied. "Everyone has the right to their own opinion."

"Then why do you fear giving your opinion?"

"I have given my opinion."

"And what is your opinion?"

"My opinion is that the United States came to Vietnam to help the South Vietnamese guarantee their right to self-determination."

Crisco sighed. "That is not what I want to hear," he said. He signaled to Spit and said something in Vietnamese. A few moments later, Spit put a tape recorder on the table. There was a reel of tape on the machine.

"It will do you no good having that machine here. I won't make a recording for you."

"Okay, okay, but I want you to listen to this."

Crisco punched a button on the machine and the tape began to turn slowly. I heard an American voice. He began to tell how we were imperialistic aggressors and how the victory of the Vietnamese people was assured. His voice was strained and he spoke in a monotone.

"Do you see?" Crisco asked, smiling at me. "One of your officers has already done this for us."

"Listen to his voice. He was forced to make this tape."

Crisco smiled at me. "You think so? Then listen to this one."

This time another voice came on. This voice wasn't strained and it didn't speak in a monotone. This American gave what amounted to an impassioned attack against the

United States for making war on the innocent civilians of Vietnam. He sounded like he meant it, really meant it, and I must confess that it shook me up pretty badly.

"Do you think this officer was forced to make this statement?" Crisco asked.

"I don't know," I admitted.

"He is a man who has truly refirmed his thinking," Crisco went on. "He has confessed that the Americans were wrong and we are right. He is genuine when he asks his fellow Americans to believe as he does."

"I don't know how you convinced him to do that for you . . . but you won't convince me."

"Oh, come now. This is not so much to ask. And your rewards are great. Think of this man. He is American like you. He is an officer like you. He is a war criminal like you. But he has repented and now he is not like you. Now he has more food than you . . . he can visit with his friends, he can play volleyball games and read books. You don't have such pleasures, do you?"

"No," I admitted.

"You could have. You can join the others. You do not have to stay alone in your cell all the time. All you have to do is make a tape for us. A simple tape."

"I wouldn't know what to say."

"We will help you," Crisco said. "We'll help you say something that is easy . . . something that won't cost you your honor . . . something you believe in. Surely you would like to see the war end so you can go home?"

"Yes, of course."

"And we want the war to end too," Crisco went on. "Perhaps you could make a statement that we both agree on."

Could I trust Crisco? If I made one little statement, what difference would it make? Several others had made the type of statement he was asking for. I had even read comments in the mimeographed newsletter attributed to well-known senators and even a former attorney general of the United States. Did they have more rights as an American citizen than I? Why could they criticize our government with impunity, whereas I as a prisoner of war would be considered a collaborator, if not a traitor, if I said the same things as they?

I decided that I wouldn't have to make it with as much enthusiasm as the one I just heard. I could make a statement like that of the first officer. No one would really believe he meant what he said when he used such words as imperialistic aggressors and peace-loving peoples. Those were typical Communist propaganda words and it was obvious his statements were forced, so what was the harm?

Oh how I longed for the sight and sound of another American. And all I had to do was agree to make this statement. It all seemed so simple and so harmless.

"Do this," Crisco cajoled, "and I will forget that you escaped. I will say that you have refirmed your thinking and have become a friend of the Vietnamese people."

Escaped.

Forget that I escaped? No, definitely not! I had found a new self-respect by my escape and I had no intention of trading that self-respect for a few more grains of rice and a little companionship. Besides, I told myself, I have all the companionship I need. I have the living Christ in my soul and Anne and my family in my heart.

"I know you are only doing your job by trying to make me do this," I said. "And I respect you for your work as an interrogator. But you must understand that I am also a good soldier and I cannot betray my country. Now let me ask you something. Suppose our positions were reversed? Suppose you were a prisoner in my country and I was the interrogator. If I asked you to make a treasonous statement against your government and against your leaders, would you?"

"No," Crisco answered resolutely.

"Why not?"

"Because I believe in my government."

"And I believe in mine," I replied. "Now, let us as two good soldiers do our duty as we see it. I will respect you for trying to get me to make a statement, but you should respect me for not making one."

Crisco looked at me for a long time and then with a grunt signaled for Spit to take me back to my cell. As we were walking away he said something to Spit. When we got back to the cell, I lay down on the solid board cot and put my legs down, waiting for the stocks to be put on. To my surprise and relief Spit picked up the stocks and left with them. Crisco had ordered them removed. I had certainly done nothing to curry his favor today. I had to believe it was because he recognized duty and honor and respected them, even if my view of duty and honor was in direct opposition to his.

This was one of the many miracles of my captivity.

13

PARIS

ANNE'S STORY

In December of 1969 the children and I were asked to join 147 other dependents and relatives of Vietnam POWs and MIAs on a trip to Paris. There we conferred with the North Vietnamese delegation at the Paris peace talks about the fate of our sons, husbands, and fathers. The trip was sponsored by the organization United We Stand, and it was financed by Ross Perot from Dallas, Texas, a very wealthy patriot who had taken a personal interest in the POW problem.

Our chartered airplane was christened *The Spirit of Christmas*. It was with exactly that hope in our hearts that we left for Paris on Christmas Eve, the second Christmas of Ben's imprisonment.

When we arrived in Paris, however, the North Vietnamese delegation was unwilling to meet with us. Three times we were told they would not meet with us because it was a holiday. Since we knew they didn't observe Christmas, we figured they were only trying to get out of the meeting. Eventually our persistence paid off, and the North Vietnamese agreed to meet with three representatives of our group.

Our representatives asked the North Vietnamese delegation to provide a complete list of all POWs being held, to arrange for their immediate release, and to accept Mr. Perot's relief plane, *Peace on Earth,* which was on its way to North Vietnam with medical and comfort supplies for the POWs.

Our appeal was answered with a twenty-five minute declamation on North Vietnamese history and policy. Despite this treatment by the North Vietnamese, we had at least been able to force them into giving us an audience by going to Paris at Christmastime with our children.

An international array of newspeople had come to watch and report on all the activities. And here, before the eyes of the entire world, were wives and children seeking word of their loved ones. Most touching were the faces of the children as they asked about their fathers. The world was watching, and North Vietnam had no choice but to respond. We felt we had won a victory. Without the generosity and backing of Ross Perot this important victory would not have been won, and those of us who suffered the long agony of having a husband, father, or son as a prisoner of war will forever be grateful for his support.

Each month I received a personal letter from the Department of the Army, telling me anything new that they might have regarding Ben or other matters pertaining to POWs and MIAs in general. They also included information that I as a POW wife might need to know.

The letters helped me to know that I wasn't forgotten by the military, and I needed that knowledge in order to keep despair from creeping back in. It kept me from feeling that I had been lost in the shuffle.

One of the letters contained information from Sybil Stockdale, the wife of Captain Jim Stockdale, a U.S. Navy pilot who was also a POW. Sybil wanted to organize a National League of Families of American POWs and MIAs in Southeast Asia. If interested, I was to write Sybil at the address given in the letter.

I was delighted! At long last, we were uniting our ranks and going public with our efforts. Until this time the government policy had been, "Keep quiet, wives and families of

POWs and MIAs," and this we had done for many years. But when we wives and families saw the war continuing and saw very little being done to get our men better treatment or to get them home, we could keep quiet no longer. It was out of this frustration that the National League of Families was born, with headquarters in Washington, D.C. The government should have known that you could keep women quiet for just so long. Sybil Stockdale quickly earned my admiration, and I was anxious for Ben to meet her when he returned home.

In May of 1970 I was flown by the Air Force to Washington for the National League organizational meeting. Many POW and MIA families attended and indicated their desire to be a part of the National League. We planned to have at least one national convention every year, but the emphasis would be on work within the area where we lived. We were to coordinate the activities of as many local areas within each state as possible. Some states had more POW and MIA families than others, but we planned to reach all areas of the country. We needed everyone's support to get public opinion to oppose North Vietnam and their policies.

Our Georgia families held their meetings about every two months. We met in Atlanta because of its central location. Millie Parrott, a POW wife, became our state coordinator. In Atlanta we heard new plans for the league as well as creative ways to get our message out to people. We didn't want our efforts to become stale and uninteresting, because we had to engage the minds of people just as willing to think about something else. Sharing ideas, news, and supportive companionship was good therapy for all of us.

Our intention was to teach the world that North Vietnam was not the innocent, humane country the war protestors kept claiming. I felt that such activists as Jane Fonda, Tom Hayden, Cora Weiss, David Dellinger, and Rennard Davis, along with some of our own senators—people like Edward Kennedy, George McGovern, William Fulbright, Eugene McCarthy, and Charles Goodell—helped to prolong the war by strengthening the will of the enemy not to negotiate.

It made me livid that citizens of our country took their freedom to dissent so far as to make it harder on our POWs.

Our men continued to languish in North Vietnamese prisons, suffering untold miseries, while a political war was being fought in Washington by people who went home every night to safe, comfortable homes. Our soldiers in Vietnam were trained, equipped, and motivated to fight, but they were prevented by politicians from getting the job done. Because we Americans have freedom of speech, we are privileged to protest, but this freedom is ours because of those who have suffered and died in wars to preserve our freedoms. With freedom come responsibilities that many protestors do not stop to consider.

I realize it is only my opinion, but for what it is worth, it is the opinion of someone who suffered through the agony of having a husband held for five years by a power hostile to the United States. War is too costly, especially in lives, to ever fight another Vietnam-type conflict. If we do not plan to fight to win, then we should not fight at all.

While in Washington for the organizational meeting, I met the family of Joe Rose and his fiancée, Donna; Michael Lenker's parents; and Robert Chenoweth's mother. Since we all had sons or husbands in the February 8 crash, it was a great reunion. Being together gave us comfort and strength, and we made plans to keep in touch.

The league helped us feel we were being heard by the people of our country as well as the government. We felt that at last we were getting the message through to everyone that our men were not being treated as they should be.

Since I could not, because of family commitments, be a national officer in the league, I decided to serve as a coordinator of the Columbus Citizens' Assistance Program, which was sponsored by the National League. We had a large committee in the Columbus area, many of whose members were military wives who assisted us with educating the public and arousing support for the POWs and MIAs. We accomplished this aim by speaking to clubs, churches, and individuals; by appearing on radio and TV; and through newspaper ads and interviews.

Doris Hill, whose husband was an MIA in Vietnam, was the other coordinator. Doris's first husband was killed in Vietnam in 1967. Two years later she married John Hill, who went to Vietnam and was reported as missing in action. Doris did not like to speak publicly, so I was often chosen to do the speaking because my husband was listed as a POW. I didn't like to speak in public either, but I did it to help our men.

I worked actively with the public, locally and statewide, to get public opinion to turn against the North Vietnamese and Viet Cong so that they would be forced to abide by the Geneva Convention. I was far from alone in this nationwide drive.

I wondered what Ben would say if he knew I had become an activist. I wondered what the North Vietnamese and Viet Cong would say about our trip and about the National League of Families. The POW families had now made so much noise in public that the enemy couldn't help but know of our activities.

Several times each month we would set up tables at shopping centers, at Fort Benning, at fairs, and at conventions, from which we could distribute bumper stickers, buttons, and information leaflets. We sold POW/MIA bracelets. Many times we had petitions and letters available for people to sign asking North Vietnam to abide by the Geneva Convention. At other times we had petitions and letters asking our congressmen and President Nixon to continue helping with the POW issue. Most of our activities were organized through the National League.

Only once was I "slapped in the face," so to speak, by callous remarks from an individual concerning POWs. It was at a local shopping center where we had a table. I saw a man approaching the table, and I remember thinking that he looked like an army sergeant, "our kind of people." As he came by the table I smiled pleasantly and asked him if he would sign our petition seeking humane treatment for our men.

"Why should I?" he asked. "They got themselves caught."

Thank goodness, experiences like that were rare.

Because Columbus, Georgia, is just outside Fort Benning, it is very much a military town, so the city was supportive in every way. The local TV stations made announcements and granted our committee members frequent on-air appearances so that we could promote the programs we were sponsoring. Griff Godwin, a local TV reporter, was especially good at providing TV coverage for our activities.

The Columbus *Ledger Enquirer,* thanks to Mr. Maynard R. Ashworth, Charles Black, and Lisa Battle, also published articles, pictures, and expensive full-page ads that helped educate the public through another medium. All of this was free of charge to our committee.

We constructed a POW cage out of bamboo. It became a part of the local parades and was used in our exhibit at the Chattahoochee Valley Fair. Each year for this fair Ryder Van Lines lent us a huge van in which we could set up our cage and distribute our information. Many people came to see what was in the van, and it gave us an opportunity to reach that many more citizens. Democratic gubernatorial candidate Jimmy Carter and his wife Rosalyn, comedian Archie Campbell, and singer-entertainer George Kirby all signed our petitions while visiting the fair. Of course this made headlines and gave us media coverage once again.

The bracelets made the POW and MIA names household words. The idea for the bracelet was conceived by Voices in Vital America, of California. VIVA, a tax-exempt, nonprofit, nonpolitical national student organization, engaged in educational programs that encouraged students to meet their obligations as citizens responsibly and within the system. Bob Hope and Martha Raye were honorary cochairmen.

The bracelets sold for $2.50. The purchaser was asked to vow that he or she would not remove it until the day the Red Cross was allowed into Hanoi so they could advise the families of POWs about the status and treatment of all our men. With the profit we made from the bracelets we printed match covers and posters to be put in public places. These items contained information about the Geneva Convention and the failure of North Vietnam to adhere to its tenets.

The money also helped us mail the numerous letters and petitions we put out for signatures. Before the bracelet sale came along as a fund-raising project, Doris and I had used our personal funds to pay for the printing and postage.

The mayor of Columbus, J. R. Allen, wore Ben's bracelet and participated in several programs throughout the city and state to support our efforts. He helped arrange a tree-planting ceremony at the City Hall in Columbus, where two Ligustrum japonicum trees were planted in honor of Ben and of Doris's husband, John. Under each tree was a bronze plaque with each man's name and the date of his disappearance.

Millie, Ben's sister, did all she could in Habersham County to inform citizens there. Banks and savings and loan associations displayed our matchbooks and leaflets for their customers.

Some milk companies put POW/MIA information on milk cartons. Bumper stickers were given out free of charge. Some were "POWs Never Have a Nice Day," "Don't Let Them Be Forgotten," "Remember the More than 1700 POWs/MIAs," and "Free POWs in Hanoi," just to name a few.

Once, the Gold Star Wives and Mothers, an organization whose members had lost a husband or son in combat, invited me to speak to their group. I arrived early and was seated in the front row in a large room. After I was introduced I walked to the podium, turned to face the group, and was shocked by the extremely large number of women who were sitting there. I was overwhelmed and had to stand there for a moment fighting back the tears. This time my sorrow was turned outward, for each of these women had lost a husband or son in war, most of them in Vietnam. Their loved ones had made the supreme sacrifice, yet here they were to hear my story and give me their support because they cared. I hope I will always remember how humble and honored I felt to be in their midst.

We had to take new and different approaches to keep our message fresh and in the minds of the public because we didn't want them to begin to ignore the problem. Sensationalism makes news, so I teased Doris, accusing her of staying up all night just so she could think up sensational things for me to do all day. Doris was a strong motivator, and we made a good team.

We heard much about the horrible food our men had to endure, especially the greasy pumpkin soup. We asked a school to prepare and serve that for lunch one day and invited the media to record the children's reactions. This event turned out to be a very effective way to get our message across, even to the children.

We also sold a POW/MIA flag, which was black with a white circle in the center. Inside the circle was the profile of a man, head slightly bent forward, with a strand of barbed wire and a prison guard tower in the background. I bought one and flew it day and night at our house.

14

THE SHINING

MOUNTAIN

BEN'S STORY

I was sitting in my cell one afternoon in May of 1970 when I heard a guard walking by, his rifle making a by now familiar sound as it hung from his shoulder and scrubbed his leg. He stopped just outside and I looked toward the door wondering if he was about to come in.

What did he want? Was I to be moved to another camp?

Suddenly something bright and shiny came skipping under the door and bounced off the back wall. Whatever it was, the guard had thrown it into my cell. Curious, I looked at it and saw that it was a piece of hard candy wrapped in gold foil.

I gasped with pleasure, unwrapped the candy and popped it into my mouth. It was good, though it had a strong strange taste. It reminded me of a little of horehound candy.

At first I planned to suck on it just a few minutes each day, thinking that I could make it last a week. Then I realized that if I did that the turnkey might find it during a search and take it away from me.

The best thing, I decided, would be to eat it all in one day, but to make it last as long as I could. I remember as a kid trying to make lemon drops last. I had developed lemon drop sucking to a fine art—no one could make a lemon drop last as long as I could. But those lemon drops were swallowed whole compared to the way I made this candy last. It was nearly dark by the time the candy was gone.

When the candy was finally gone, I looked at the piece of gold paper that had been the wrapping. I realized then that I was getting a bonus. The cell I was in was a featureless white. The ceiling and walls were whitewashed and the floor was gray concrete. I didn't realize until I had that piece of gold foil what a debilitating effect this sterile atmosphere had been having on me.

I took the gold foil, fashioned it in the shape of a mountain, and hung it on the wall just underneath the new bamboo cross I had made. I wanted something—anything—to break up the sterility of the room.

It was beautiful. I watched the light play upon it and then split off into little golden beams. Because of the cross, I could make this mountain of gold foil into the hill of Calvary and with very little imagination see the crucifixion as it must have been played out almost two thousand years ago. I know it is difficult to understand, but a twenty-three-inch color TV couldn't give the average American more pleasure than that little piece of foil was giving me. Sometimes I would put my hands around my eyes, like blinders, and slowly sweep my gaze across the wall until the gold foil came into view. I would watch it in the evening until the light was too dim to see and be greeted by it in the morning when the room grew light.

My mood began to pick up. Then, two months after I put the piece of foil on the wall, a turnkey entered my cell and removed both the foil and the cross from my wall. I was devastated. Why did they take them away? What possible harm could a little piece of foil and a bamboo cross be?

I lay on my bunk for the rest of the day mourning the loss of my "interest center." I was very depressed and broke down in tears. Right away I told myself that this was getting out of hand. There was no way I was going to make it through my ordeal if I let everything affect me as this loss had. I had to do something positive to help my own cause, so I decided to go on a hunger strike.

I knew by this time that the Vietnamese would lose face if one of their prisoners died by starvation. They had locked my legs in stocks and had let injuries and ailments go untreated, but I must confess that they always fed me an adequate, though boring, diet. With whatever convoluted logic it was that guided them, they could better explain a death from beating than one from starvation. Knowledge of this gave me a weapon to use against them.

I also knew that I now had the strength to go on a hunger strike. I could go quite a while without food if I had water to drink. But the guards had learned how to deal with a hunger strike by taking away my water whenever I refused to eat the food provided. Without water, two previous hunger strikes I had attempted had lasted for only five days each.

This was Sunday, and as a sign of protest I did not accept either of the two meals offered to me that day. As I expected, Crisco summoned me to the interrogation room early on Monday.

"Why do you not eat?"

"I'm despondent," I replied. "The turnkey removed the cross from my cell. You promised me I could have that cross."

Crisco frowned and said, "Go back to your cell and eat. I will check on the cross."

I had learned long ago that to obtain any consideration of my requests at all, I must be willing to meet the Vietnamese partway. They absolutely must have some way to save face. So I agreed to eat.

I ate both meals on Monday and Tuesday, and then early Wednesday morning Crisco summoned me to the interrogation room again. As I entered the room I noticed that Spit was also with Crisco. Following a few meaningless remarks, Crisco departed the room. Spit and I stared at each other for a short while.

"Who is the pope?" he asked.

I was surprised by the question. "What? Well, I don't really know. I don't know who the pope is."

"You don't know?" Spit asked suspiciously.

"No."

"But aren't you Catholic?"

"No." It was apparent to me then that Spit, a Vietnamese Communist, thought all Christians were Catholics.

"If you are not Catholic, why do you want the cross in your cell?"

I tried to explain to Spit, as I had earlier to Crisco, that the empty cross was a symbol of faith for the Southern Baptist, whereas the Catholic crucifix has an image of Christ on it.

Spit seemed to understand a bit more than Crisco about our faith and about Christianity, but he floored me with his next statement. "But Christians don't lie, and we now know you lied to us back at Bao Cao."

That was the first reference they had ever made to the "zone defense" interrogation. Also, I was bemused by his apparent belief that Christians don't lie. How wonderful it would be if that were true.

The incident ended when Crisco returned.

"You can have the cross back but you cannot have that piece of paper," he said.

I realized that he was compromising with me and saving face for the turnkey who had taken my gold foil. Despite the loss of my gold foil the entire episode raised my spirits. I felt that I had won another victory.

15

THE CHILDREN OF

WAITING WIVES

ANNE'S STORY

In 1971 the time arrived for Joy, our youngest child, to enter kindergarten. She had been only twenty months old when Ben had left for Vietnam. Now she was five-and-a-half years old. Ben was missing so much of our children's lives . . . their fun, accomplishments, and growing pains. I savored each accomplishment, hoping I would remember them all so that if Ben came home at the end of the war I could share them with him.

I dreaded Joy's first day of kindergarten. It wasn't that I was sad she was going to school, but because there was rarely any place I went that she didn't go, I was afraid she wouldn't let me leave her at kindergarten. However, the morning we walked into her classroom and saw her teacher, Joy turned to me and said, "She looks like Meme."

Meme is what she called my mother. I breathed a sigh of relief and told her I would meet her outside the classroom door after school. I watched as she sat down in her assigned seat, and when I turned to walk away I heard absolutely no sound of protest. I knew then that all was well.

Joy was very grown up, much older than her young years. I believe it must have been the influence of the adult company she always had. She was a very pretty little girl and extremely smart. Her teachers always gave me good reports about her.

Sherri had started to school the year we moved back to Columbus. She was also happy in school. We lived close to South Columbus Elementary School, and the children were able to walk to school every day. Sherri walked until she got her bike, and then that became her transportation to school and her enjoyment at home. Her hair was platinum blond, the shade of Ben's childhood cotton-top. I could always count on her soft, sweet smile to lift my spirits.

David attended Baker High School about six blocks from our house. When we bought our house in the fifties, we were fortunate enough to choose one in an area that was convenient for schools and shopping. I wished with all my heart Ben could see this good-looking young man. With his bright blue eyes and a sugar-bowl dimple in his chin, he reminded me of his father. I knew, however, that Ben would not have cared much for the long hair that was the style of the day.

David was on the debate team and worked hard preparing his part. He was active in the church youth group and enjoyed lots of activities with them. For extra money he mowed yards for our neighbors.

When David turned sixteen he asked for a car. Ben and I had never talked about buying a car for any of our children. They had been too young for cars when Ben left. I wasn't sure how Ben would feel about this request.

When I made decisions I found that I second-guessed myself, wondering how Ben would feel about them. However, I was now alone and the decisions were mine to make, good or bad. My decision this time was to buy a light blue Volkswagen for David.

In order to support the car, David now needed more money than grass cutting could provide, so he took a job at a putt-putt course near our house. I was happy to see that he had inherited his dad's work habits: I received reports on the good job he was doing and his dedication to it.

David also had excellent study habits and was inducted into the National Honor Society during his junior year in high school. I was a proud mother at the honors banquet, with one regret—that Ben wasn't there to share the special moment. I knew Ben would approve of David's diligence.

At the beginning of his senior year, David applied for an appointment to West Point and the Air Force Academy as well as for an ROTC scholarship. Considering that in the late sixties having anything to do with the military was very unpopular with the young people of our country, I was surprised that David would consider these options. However, I was pleased that he did. He seemed to feel that by doing this he was honoring his father, perhaps helping him in some way. He received answers to all three applications in the same mail. He had an appointment to West Point, got an ROTC scholarship, and was second alternate for an Air Force Academy appointment.

Once again it was decision time. He asked my advice, but I refused to give my preference, only asking him to consider the opportunities seriously and thoroughly before making his choice. I felt this had to be his decision and his alone. David wished his dad was available to discuss options, for his future depended upon the decision he made now. In late spring he accepted the appointment to West Point. I was glad he had made this choice; I felt he needed mature male influence which had been missing from his life all through his high school years.

His graduation was held in the Columbus city auditorium because his class was so large, about eight times the size of my high school graduating class in Baldwin, Georgia. We had a pregraduation party for him with family and friends. Walter and Janet Cook came from Atlanta to attend the party and the graduation with us. Walter, Ben's closest friend as far back as high school, seemed the logical person to share this special event with us, although nothing could really compensate for Ben's absence.

In mid-June David left for West Point to attend Beast Barracks, the summer training program. Just the name of the training session made me wince as I wondered what he would be going through. I wished Ben was here to reassure me that David would be okay.

For the last two years before David went to college, I had prepared myself for his leaving the nest and I felt I had been brave for a mother seeing her first-born leave home. I couldn't afford the luxury of tears over his leaving. I had to be strong or his going would be too painful to bear, but very often I wanted to cry. I needed to turn him loose but found that, especially under the circumstances, it was very difficult for me to do so. I wished I could cling to Ben. I knew I'd feel better if I could.

Our oldest daughter, Debbie, had grown into an exceptionally pretty young lady with blue eyes and blond hair. She took music lessons and had a beautiful singing voice. I used to wonder whom she got that from. I remembered Ben telling me the story of his asking a voice teacher to give him singing lessons. After the teacher heard Ben sing a scale he replied, "You'd best forget about singing lessons, son."

Debbie sang in a chorus, beginning in junior high, and was chosen to be a member of All-State Chorus for three years in a row. To go to All-State she had to learn many difficult pieces of music as well as compete in several auditions.

Debbie was always very aware of Ben's situation and read a great deal about the plight of our POWs and about the war. In one of her sixth-grade classes the students had to write a paper about their feelings on the bombing halt. The writer of the best paper would be given a Japanese sword. Debbie expressed her agreement with the bombing halt ordered by President Nixon. She stated,

When President Johnson stopped the bombing in North Vietnam, many people thought it was just a political move for the Democratic Party. I agree with this for one reason. The bombing halt was advised months before it was carried out and should have been done before the final campaign hours. Had this been done sooner, it would not have appeared to be a political move.

With a new president and the bombing halt, maybe the Viet Cong will join in the peace talks and progress can be made . . .

Debbie won the award. I'm sure there was no one in her class who could come close to being as qualified as she was to write that particular paper. At the age of eleven she was aware of the political impact of the war. She knew it was being fought in Washington by politicians and not on the battlefields of Vietnam by the military commanders. This was not what an eleven-year-old girl should have to think about. Her days should be carefree and happy before the responsibilities of adult life come along.

Upon finishing at Eddy Junior High, Debbie received the Manton Sprague Eddy Award, the highest award for scholastic achievements and leadership ability given at the school. Being there to see her accept this honor was another proud moment in my life.

Debbie entered the Columbus School's science fair and won first place in her school in the social science division and the next year first place in the zoology division. In both events she won third place in city-wide competition.

I was greatly pleased to see how interested Debbie was in our church activities. She was president of the Church Youth Council for two years, and during the summer she attended church camps and retreats. One year she attended a three-week Super Summer retreat at Furman University, sponsored by the Home Mission Board of the Southern Baptist Convention. Debbie was always a good student and enjoyed doing her very best in whatever she undertook. She had spunk and drive just like her dad, which I admired and which I hoped she would never lose.

Cliff did okay in school. He made passing grades without much effort but enjoyed having fun as he went along. Cliff was the blithe spirit of our family. He was the one who always kept us laughing. We especially needed that in our lives. The fun and laughter he brought into our family served as a bonding and healing process.

I always cut Cliff's hair. Once I cut it too short and when he looked into the mirror he cried and said, "Nobody's going to love me now."

When long hair became the fad he fussed so much about my cutting his hair that I finally stopped being his barber. After that he wore his hair much longer than I liked, and I was sure Ben would feel the same way. But his character traits were good, and that was more important to me than worrying about the length of his hair. I felt that someday he would get a haircut and when the girls were able to see how good-looking he really was he would break a few hearts.

Cliff played Little League baseball from the time he first became eligible. His best friend, Nicky Garbarino, played on the same team, and Nicky's dad, Major Garbarino, coached the team. Cliff was the catcher. He was an excellent player and enjoyed the game so much that I wondered if he might someday make baseball his career. Playing ball was an outlet for Cliff. It helped him expend a great deal of pent-up energy in a wholesome atmosphere. He said that when he played ball he didn't have to think about his dad. His young mind was searching for something fun to replace his sadness.

Cliff was chosen as captain of the safety patrol at school and one summer went with the patrol by train to Washington, D.C. This gave him an opportunity to tour our nation's capital and learn a little history at the same time. He had a great time riding the train and visiting the city.

Not to be outdone by his sister Debbie, Cliff entered the social science fair at his school and won first place. He also took up bowling during the season when he wasn't playing baseball. He was on a Saturday league, and before long he was scoring over 200! Ben always liked to bowl, and I could see competition between father and son in the future if Ben made it home. That would be fun to see. I wondered if Ben could visualize leaving a seven-year-old son and coming home to a son who might possibly beat him in bowling?

Seeing the determination of our children to accomplish all these things, despite our uncertain existence, made me very proud of each of them. I knew they were all hurting in their own way and didn't know how to express their pain in words or how to relieve their hurt. I encouraged and helped the children all I could, and they knew I was proud of them. They were my reason for living, for going on and leading as normal a life as we could. My job, my privilege, was to raise them to be good men and women who loved God and tried to live by the example Jesus gave us. When they received awards and recognition I was there beaming with pride for both myself and their dad, but I wanted to cry when I thought of Ben's having to miss so much of their growing-up years. I was sure that if Ben was alive he was having these same regrets.

Not knowing what lay ahead in my own future, I decided that I had better prepare myself for the work force in the event Ben didn't return. It had been a long time since I had worked as a secretary in an office. In fact, I had never even typed on an electric typewriter. To prepare myself, I enrolled at Columbus Vocational Tech and attended classes two nights a week studying typing and business English. The classes gave me a social outlet with adults as well as being educationally beneficial.

I also became active in the Waiting Wives Club. There were hundreds of wives in the Columbus area whose husbands were overseas—in Vietnam or other countries. The club gave us an opportunity to share experiences; provided fellowship, fun, and support; and helped us realize that we weren't alone. Several times we were on a local television show, *The Rosell Show,* to advertise our Waiting Wives Club. That was a very interesting experience for all of us. Our children always appeared on the show with us, and Joy decided then, even at her young age, to be in TV communications when she grew up.

In 1971 I was chosen as Fort Benning's Army Wife of the Year and felt extremely honored to hold such a title. My name had been submitted by the Waiting Wives Club. Entrants were judged on community service.

Through the years as a military wife I had held many volunteer positions in the community, such as Cub Scout leader, assistant Brownie leader, school grade mother, sponsor for Allied students (military students from our allied countries who came to U.S. military posts for training), thrift shop volunteer, member of parent-teacher associations, president of the Waiting Wives Club, member of the Officer's Wives Club, cochairman of the Columbus Citizens' Assistance Program for prisoners of war, and president of my church Woman's Missionary Union, and I had been active in my church as teacher, pianist, and Girls In Action leader.

I felt living day-to-day among civilians, participating in

their activities, and being their friend showed them that the military wife has the same desires and goals in life as they have. The civilians could see that I did not desire to be a burden to the community but a help to them. They accepted me as their friend, and then I was able to help them better understand military life. I feel that working, playing, and praying together is the best way to better relations between American military and civilian communities.

Columbus was a wonderful community to live in. They gave us their love and support, and we did our best to respond by being an active part of the community.

I didn't find very many things to laugh about in those days, except when I was with three very dear friends: Margaret Thomas, Ethel Burgamy, and Irene Thornell. When we met for lunch or a shopping trip, laughter was the order of the day. After an outing with them I always felt like the earth must feel after a soft, cooling rain. My soul was refreshed. When we were together we found humor in everything. I didn't know I needed that laughter, but God knew and he provided it for me. Another lesson learned: Bring laughter into the lives of those who hurt.

16

HANDSHAKE

One night in early November of 1970 I heard SAM missiles being fired about ten miles away. The next day there was a great deal of activity in the camp. The turnkeys, who had not been wearing sidearms for several months, suddenly began wearing them again. Trustee prisoners, under the supervision of guards, began digging foxholes . . . very deep foxholes. After that, about once each month, whistles would blow, all the lights within the compound would go out, and all the Vietnamese would scurry about and jump into the foxholes. The POWs were left in their cells.

It wasn't long after I heard the SAMs being fired before Crisco called me out for another session.

"How is your health?" he asked.

"Okay, as far as I know."

Crisco picked up a thermos of hot water and poured it over something that appeared to be tea leaves. A moment later, when the water had barely changed color, he poured it into a very small cup and handed it to me.

"Have some tea," he invited.

"Thank you."

Taking a sip of tea, Crisco stared at me over the rim of his cup. Finally, after smacking his lips appreciatively, he set the cup down on the table and wiped his lips with the back of his hand.

"Tell me. Do you think the Americans will invade North Vietnam?"

"I don't know," I answered with tongue in cheek. "There's really no telling what those crazy Americans will do if you make them mad enough." I wanted him to worry about the possibility of some form of action by U.S. Forces.

Crisco took another swallow of his tea. "Your wife," he said.

My ears perked up and I looked at him curiously. What was he about to say about Anne?

"Do you think she is involved in any of the public demonstrations that are taking place all over America?"

I smiled and shook my head.

"No," I replied. "Absolutely not. She is a loving mother and housewife. She would never become involved in any kind of political activity."

He took my cup from me. "Go back to your cell," he said.

It wasn't until the truce was declared in January 1973 and I was transferred to the Hao Loa prison (better known as the Hanoi Hilton) that I learned of the events that led up to the frantic activities at K-77. I learned that Crisco's curiosity and the periodic alert exercises of the guards were brought on by the attempt of American forces to rescue the prisoners held at Son Tay, a suspected prisoner-of-war complex located about twenty miles to the west of Hanoi.

Every morning as part of my responsibilities I was obliged to sweep out my cell. There was a gap of about four inches between the bottom of the door and the floor, and I would sweep the trash through the gap into the hallway. A prisoner trustee, perhaps a South Vietnamese soldier who had "refirmed his thinking" in order to have the opportunity to work outside his cell, would then sweep the trash out of the hallway and into a larger trash pile outside the building.

One morning just after I had finished with the sweeping and had sat back down on my cot, I saw the trash that I had just pushed into the hallway being swept back into my cell. Thinking the trustee had made a simple mistake, I got up and swept the trash back outside. Within seconds the trash was swept under my door again, and I simply swept it back out. When the trustee started sweeping the trash back into my cell a third time I got a little upset. I walked over to the door, got down on my hands and knees, and watched. As soon as the broom came toward me I reached under the door and grabbed it.

"*Khom*," the trustee called, meaning "no." He pulled back on the broom but I held onto it.

Although he didn't say anything else, he was beginning to get a little frightened. I could tell that by the anxious way he was pulling on the broom. And when I thought about it I knew he had a right to be a little frightened. If he lost the broom or was caught making contact with one of the American prisoners, he would probably be punished. At the minimum he would lose his privileged status as a trustee. I thought about that for a moment and then let go of the broom.

The trustee pulled his broom back, then stuck his hand under the door, slapped his palm on the floor once, and offered it to me in the form of a handshake. I reached out to shake his hand. Suddenly I realized that this was the first time in over three years that I had touched another human being in friendship.

Overcome by this show of friendship I held his hand for a long moment and even put my other hand over his, savoring this bit of human contact. I think he must have known that I was the American who had been in solitary confinement for thirty-eight months, because he made no effort to pull his hand away. Instead he, too, stuck his other hand under the door and patted my hand as one would when comforting a friend.

I was deeply moved by this man's simple act of compassion, and I shall never forget it so long as I live. If losing his broom would have gotten him in trouble, think how much more trouble he would have been in had he been caught comforting me. And yet he made no effort to pull his hand away. Instead, he seemed perfectly willing to run the risk of being caught just to let me savor the moment. Finally, I realized that I had to let go and with one final squeeze I did so.

I walked over to my bunk and sat down to think about what had just happened. I had not seen the face of that man. I assumed he was a South Vietnamese trustee, but they also had North Vietnamese civil prisoners in the same compound, and it could have been one of them. Whoever it was, I loved him with all the strength of love for humanity there was in me.

I am not ashamed to say that I wept. But the tears I shed were tears of thankfulness. The Lord had sent that prisoner to me to let me know that I was not alone, and it was as though the Lord himself had touched me.

After the handshake my whole day seemed brighter. The food seemed better, the guards acted more decently, and I had no trouble thinking happy thoughts. To top everything else, shortly after that I had the first really good laugh I had enjoyed since my capture. Of course, I had to wait until I was back in my cell before I could let it out, but I enjoyed it immensely. Just as the Lord had sent me the Vietnamese to touch, he provided me with this laugh.

It happened during a brainwashing session with Crisco. He had called me out into the courtyard, and we were sitting across a small table from each other. He was giving me the same line he had used so many times before, trying to get me to refirm my thinking, to confess my crimes against the Vietnamese people and admit that the United States was conducting an unlawful war. And, as usual, I was refusing to go along with it.

The truth is, although I would never have let Crisco know, I had actually come to enjoy these interrogations, especially when they were conducted outside. It gave me a few precious moments of the illusion of freedom. It was a very pretty day, the sun was shining brightly, the trees were waving in the breeze, the prison-yard chickens were walking around clucking contentedly. I could have been sitting in the front yard of a farmhouse back in Georgia. About half of my consciousness was enjoying the pleasant outside atmosphere while the other half paid just enough attention to Crisco to answer his questions.

"You are being foolish," Crisco said. "You will never get out of here. We will charge you with crimes against the Vietnamese people and you will stay in our prison for the rest of your life."

"You won't do that."

"Oh? Do you know who Rudolph Hess is?"

"Yes, of course I do. He is a Nazi war criminal."

Crisco smiled. "Yes. He is a war criminal imprisoned in Spandau Prison and he has been there since the end of World War II. We can do the same thing to you."

"No, you can't. I am not a war criminal."

"We say that you are."

"My government will have something to say about that."

"Your government? Your government?" Crisco shouted. He stood up and pounded on the table, then leaned over so that his face was just inches from mine. He yelled, "Do you think your government cares about you? Do you think they even know you are here? Look around you. What do you see? You see Vietnamese soldiers, that's who you see. You see Vietnamese guns, Vietnamese barbed wire. The only other Americans here are helpless criminals just like you. If your government is so concerned, why isn't someone here to help you right now?"

At that very moment, as if it had been a player waiting offstage for his cue, an F-4 Phantom jet flashed by overhead, so low that it blocked out the sun. Both afterburners were lit, and the plane was going so fast that we saw it, and then it was gone—all in absolute, eerie silence.

A split-second later the sound exploded over us. Ten times louder than the loudest roar of thunder, it broke windows and rattled the very walls of the prison. It was so sudden and unexpected that Crisco literally screamed in fear and surprise. All over the compound guards turned ashen-faced and dived for cover, so afraid were they of our airplanes.

I sat perfectly still and didn't say a word, but Crisco could read the expression on my face. Where are they now? my expression said. They are right here!

When Crisco finally regained his composure, he ran a visibly shaking hand through his hair and looked at me.

"Go . . . go back to your cell," he said in a strangely subdued voice.

I laughed about that incident for over an hour. It sure felt good to laugh again. I had not realized how much I had missed laughing until that very moment.

After the F-4 incident Crisco left me alone for several days. Then he summoned me for another interrogation. When I sat down I saw that there was an empty teacup sitting on the table between us. The teacup, blue on cream, had rather pretty designs painted on all sides. Crisco reached down to the cup and began rotating it slowly on the table, doing it very methodically so as to get my attention. He got it, because I watched intently.

"I want you to notice the designs on this cup," he said, his quiet, sibilant voice sliding out as smooth as oil. This wasn't his intimidating tone . . . this was his persuasive tone. "If you will notice, you will see something different when you look at the other side. Like this cup, the Vietnamese war has many sides. But you stubbornly refuse to see our side." He looked up at me with a smug smile on his face. "You have not refirmed your thinking."

I was very surprised by this particular analogy. To understand what was so unusual about this experience one would have to know what I did during a brainwashing session Crisco conducted several months earlier, on September 2, 1969.

At that time I had been thinking of some way to counter Crisco's demands that I refirm my thinking, and I came up with what I thought was a novel idea. While at the washing place one day I picked up a piece of paper from an empty cigarette package and prepared it so as to illustrate my point that there were several ways to look at the Vietnamese conflict.

My training aid is hard to describe verbally, so let me draw the following crude sketch:

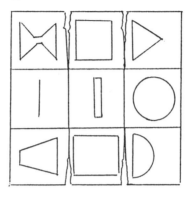

Note: Tears indicate the paper was folded several ways and could be opened (i.e., third dimension revealed) one square at a time.

I uncovered the center square and said, "I am showing you two dimensions of a three-dimensional object. From seeing only two sides, can you tell me what the object is?"

Crisco looked interested but didn't respond.

I uncovered in succession each of the surrounding squares, all of which contained a possible third dimension of the center drawing. "You see," I said, "the object could be a coin, a wedge, a key, a square box, a rectangular box, a thin sheet of paper, or any of several oddly shaped items.

"Now I have seen one side of this conflict with my own eyes—I've listened to my government's announcements on why we are involved in Vietnam and I accept them as valid. And I've listened to you explain the Vietnamese government's position on many occasions, so you see, I know more about the facts of this war than you do. However, I'm certain there are many sides of this war that neither you nor I know about, and therefore the total truth escapes us both."

As Crisco was beginning to respond, our session was interrupted by Spit. He walked over to Crisco and whispered something in his ear. Crisco turned pale as a ghost and ended our conversation abruptly. It was several days later before I learned that Spit had informed Crisco that Ho Chi Minh had just died.

On that occasion I had been denied the opportunity to engage Crisco in a meaningful discussion of our respective views, but from what he was doing now with the designs on the teacup I was confident that at least one of my points had not been lost on him.

After more than three years as a prisoner I was honestly beginning to wonder if I would ever be free again. I was frustrated by the Paris peace talks; the propaganda newsletter circulated periodically was certainly not very encouraging. Still, I had some hope that peace would come soon, but that hope grew dimmer with each passing day.

In addition to the depression, I began to experience several other health problems. I suffered constantly from diarrhea, which sometimes turned to dysentery and which sapped what little energy I received from the boring diet. (Boiled cabbage, bread, and hot water was our meal fifty times in January of 1970.) Also each fall as the weather turned cold I could count on a case of sinusitis.

I had somehow become accustomed to all of the ailments until a new one hit me. I developed a kidney stone. I could not urinate for three days. The pressure on my bladder and kidneys became very intense and the pain was unbearable. I asked Crisco to send for a doctor. In the meanwhile he gave me a small vial of ointment, much like mentholatum, and told me to rub it on my stomach and back until the doctor could come.

Near nightfall of the third day I had a strong urge to use the toilet bucket. I heard a noise like a stone hitting the bucket and immediately felt relief. The kidney stone had passed of its own accord. That night I slept soundly for the first time in seventy-two hours.

Three days later Crisco summoned me to the small room where medical supplies were stored. A *bac si* was waiting there to examine me. When I told him I no longer had a problem he became very irate and said I shouldn't have wasted his time.

As I think back on it, I'm probably lucky the *bac si* wasn't available on the first or second day. There's no telling what treatment he might have prescribed.

17

PROBLEMS

Through the many long months of our ordeal there were several frustrations that I remember. I feel blessed now to have survived without being devoured by depression and despair.

A few days after Ben's capture, my mother flew out to be with us. On Easter Sunday that first year, a severe pain in her upper left side sent me scurrying with her to the hospital. There we discovered she had a staph infection in her lung. For ten days her doctor could not find an antibiotic that would curb the infection. In fact, one day when I went to visit her Dr. Draper met me in the hallway and asked if I would go with him to the coffee shop for a cup of coffee. As we sat talking he said, "Anne, your mother is a very sick woman."

The remark didn't sink into my mind as he intended. It was some months later before I realized that he had been trying to prepare me for the very likely possibility that my mother would die from the infection. I did not even consider that possibility. I wasn't in touch with reality at that time.

Once her doctor found a medicine that would help she began to respond immediately, but the illness had taken its toll. Even after she was well enough to travel back to Georgia, it took her a year to get over her depression and regain her strength. I'm sure much of her depression was a result of our situation.

Debbie, too, had difficulty adjusting to Ben's status. One year near Christmas she became convinced that we would be receiving a letter from him. She got this idea because Cora Weiss and David Dellinger, antiwar activists and members of the New Mobilization Committee, had gone to Hanoi to show solidarity with the North Vietnamese in protesting our country's participation in the war.

Supposedly as a humanitarian gesture, but in reality adding to the frustration of the POW and MIA families, these activists always brought back three or four letters from POWs. Then they used their propaganda through the news media to try to convince the American people that North Vietnam was being lenient by letting the POWs write and also that they were treating our prisoners well.

I did not like to think our news media agreed with this group. I preferred to think they didn't really know how our men were suffering and that they were merely being used by these people. I despised the lies the New Mobilization Committee forced our POW and MIA families to endure. Their visits to North Vietnam only added more pain and more doubt.

Despite all of this, and despite my warning to her, Debbie started meeting the mailman every afternoon expecting that long-awaited letter. My heart would break as I watched her wait and then saw her face fall when the mailman did not bring the letter she so desperately hoped to receive. My disappointments hurt me, but to see our children hurt was almost more pain than I could bear.

There were other things, small things that always happened when the soldier goes away. Mechanical things, for example, seem to have some innate sense of knowing that the man of the house is gone so now is the time to break. The handle to our refrigerator had just been repaired before Ben left. When we moved to Columbus, however, it broke again, and I had to keep a crowbar handy just to be able to open it while we waited for our new refrigerator to arrive.

Bob Whitt, my neighbor, taught me how to light the furnace pilot light and the gas water heater which always managed to blow out when we had a big wind storm. I had to have a new sewer pipe put in because tree roots had grown into the old one. Then I had to put a new roof and fascia boards on the house, enlarge the storage room, and add a few more cabinets in the kitchen. It seemed that something always needed fixing!

One day a man from Orkin pest control found some termites, which had to be treated through the inside wall in our den. That left an unsightly hole in the den wall, so David and I decided it could be best repaired by putting up paneling. David proved to be quite a handyman, like Ben. He did the work himself and it looked great. David remembered some of the things Ben had taught him and always tried to help with repairs.

We had large oak trees outside the house. The children and I raked leaves all fall and winter and into spring until the new ones arrived. In the fall we had to start the cycle all over again. This was a chore all of us hated, but it did provide time together as we raked, bagged the leaves, and grumbled.

Shortly after returning to Georgia I bought a new car. We had been planning to buy one as soon as Ben returned, and I felt that having a new car would at least free me of car worries. That wasn't actually true. Something was always happening—flat tires, alternator going out, fan belts breaking, et cetera. Always before whenever Ben left, the car was the thing that most intimidated me because I knew so little about it. My past experience with a car had only been to make sure there was gas in the tank. But I soon learned that there is much more than gas that keeps a car running.

After four years the car paint was beginning to fade, so I had it repainted. I went for the car late one afternoon and the next morning realized what a terrible job they had done. The car felt gritty all over. By now I had learned to be more assertive than I once was and I took it back to them, insisting they do it over. They confessed the water had gone off while preparing the car and thus the grit effect. I was angry they had tried to pass it off as a good job.

One day Sherri and I were at Fort Benning and a woman

backed into the right side of our car. It was the woman's sixtieth birthday, and she was in a hurry to get home for a party. We were shaken up but not hurt. The repairs took two weeks to complete. If her insurance company had not permitted us to rent a car at their expense, I don't know how we would have managed to get around.

I have gone through this litany of problems only to show that the normal routine of living had to go on, forcing me to do alone those things for which I had always depended upon Ben.

There were also problems with children "coming of age." One night David went to spend the night with his friend Mike Waugh. During the night I awoke with a start and a very uneasy feeling about David. I slipped out of bed and huddled in a corner near a heater vent to keep warm, trying to fight this uneasiness and praying that he was all right. Finally I was able to go back to bed.

Without my knowledge or permission David and Mike had decided to make a quick trip to Daytona Beach to see a friend of Mike's. I later learned they had planned to do this within a twenty-four-hour time frame. At 6:00 A.M. the phone rang. It was David informing me he had fallen asleep at the wheel of his VW, run off the right side of the road, gone down an embankment, and flipped the car end over end.

The VW was a total loss but David and Mike had only a few bruises and scratches. I was very displeased he had gone without permission but relieved and thankful that he was okay. David didn't have a car for the last two months of his senior year in high school, which seemed to be punishment enough for a young man his age.

Through the Waiting Wives Club I met many wives who became my close friends. One friend, Frances Payne, was expecting her husband home from Vietnam. When a husband was coming home all of us in our club rejoiced with the wife.

Frances's husband was in the Ordnance Branch as a demolition expert. As a precautionary measure for the last month before rotation home, he had been taken off duty. One day he went with a friend to disarm a rocket. He was just a bystander, but the rocket exploded unexpectedly and Frances's husband was killed.

This was a devastating blow for all of our close-knit group. We had just celebrated his impending homecoming with her. Now we suffered with Frances and her family. Having seen them so close to reunion only to be separated forever left all of us shaken and sad. The funeral, held in a small chapel at Fort Benning, was one of the saddest I had ever attended.

The army takes care of its own, so the saying goes, but there were times early on when I felt this wasn't happening. When I tried to join the Fort Benning Officers' Club, I was told that because I claimed my husband was MIA I would have to get official documents to prove his status. This infuriated me. I wondered how many wives came to the club office and claimed their husbands were MIA so that they could join the Officers' Club. Surely a simple phone call on their part could have verified my claim. I found it humiliating that they would imply I might lie about such a thing.

Another frustration of dealing with the army was that our Citizen's Assistance Organization had to go through a lot of red tape. For example, we had to type up our request and make certain we used exactly the right words, such as table and not booth, just to get permission to distribute our leaflets and bumper stickers at Fort Benning. It was obvious that the post commander and his advisors did not know us well or he would have known we would never do anything inappropriate on post. We definitely needed more personal dialogue with those in charge at Fort Benning. I was beginning to get the impression we weren't welcome on the military post. Those who, I thought, should care the most seemed to care very little.

In April 1971 Iris Powers, an MIA mother who was conducting a nationwide tour of army installations on behalf of General Westmoreland, arrived at Fort Benning. I was invited to attend a meeting she had with the Personnel Actions Branch, where she reviewed what was being done to assist POW and MIA dependents in the local area. During the meeting I said I felt that General Talbott, the Commanding General of Fort Benning, had not made our committee feel welcome on the post and had often given us the impression he wished we would just go away. This was enough said to get the senior officers busy correcting the problem.

After Mrs. Powers's visit many changes were made. Fort Benning now welcomed us enthusiastically; they couldn't do enough for us. The military had learned how *better* to take care of its own. I wish we had been welcomed this way earlier.

Selena Murdock became the post coordinator and coordinated our Fort Benning activities with ease and full cooperation. I had not enjoyed struggling with the military and found comfort in knowing we were at last working together.

I came to realize that it wasn't *what* one had to face that was important but *how* one faced it that mattered. I hope I will always remember this.

18

SNOOPY AND ON'

BEN'S STORY

There was one interesting turnkey I dubbed Snoopy who had been around K-77 for several months before my escape attempt in 1969. Most of the time he left me alone, but occasionally he would slip up to my cell door and look in quickly in an attempt to catch me doing something out of line—hence his title. Snoopy became one of the victims of my escape.

Just a few days before the escape Snoopy pulled a very superficial inspection of my cell and found only one item of contraband, which he immediately confiscated: a small comb I had made out of bamboo. Although it wasn't a masterpiece by any means, it had served a useful purpose and I hated to lose it.

The next morning Snoopy was standing just outside my cell when he pulled the comb from his rear pocket, looked at it with contempt, and then said, *"Khom tot, khom tot."* "Not good, not good." Then he tossed it over the prison wall. I suppose I must have given him a dirty look for he immediately entered my cell and proceeded to inspect everything very thoroughly—or so he thought. Snoopy never looked under the cot closely enough to find the handmade chisel, which was cradled in a piece of toilet paper tied to a bed slat. And he didn't notice a black string lying on the floor near the door. Had he stooped to pick up the string, he would have pulled my drill out of the cavity formed from a rotting door jamb.

I dared not breathe a sigh of relief too soon, for those items paled in comparison to what he would have found had he looked behind the cell door opened inward against the wall. By then my work was nearly done and the panel was being held in place by a single sliver of wood!

Snoopy had departed my cell with an obvious feeling of superiority, for he had "shown that insolent American just who was boss." Little did he suspect that within three days that insolent American would succeed in embarrassing not only him but the entire camp hierarchy by getting out of the cell and going over the wall.

After my recapture and return to K-77 on the morning of December 8 Snoopy came by my cell only once. His eyes shot me full of daggers and he made it rather clear that he hated my guts. I only smiled inwardly and felt somewhat vindicated, for I was at that moment his equal.

Seven months went by before I saw Snoopy again. He suddenly reappeared at K-77 in mid-July 1970. I felt a little apprehensive at seeing him again and wondered what he would do.

By this time I had become somewhat complacent and was perhaps a little careless in my efforts to conceal two items which were symbolic to my program of resistance—a splinter of wood and a homemade flag.

In the waistband of my trousers I carried the last splinter of wood removed from the door of cell 18 prior to my escape. I also carried a small American flag I had made as evidence that I was an American serviceman and not a spy. I wanted to bring these items home as souvenirs.

When Snoopy unlocked my cell one morning to allow me out to empty the toilet bucket and wash my face, I had no idea what he had in mind. When I returned to my cell a few moments later I noticed several items lying in a chair outside my cell: the flag, the strip of wood, and several small crosses shaped from soup bone, plus a razor blade which had been an inadvertent extra in the blade wrapper I had received several months before. It was a very thorough inspection indeed, and it led me to believe that Snoopy had been away for six months just to learn how to inspect a prisoner's cell!

Our relationship rocked along on an uneven course until midsummer 1971. Then sometime late in July 1971 Snoopy let me out of my cell for my fresh air and exercise period. As I stood in the warm sunshine, loosening up my stiff and aching back, Snoopy sat in a chair under a shade tree.

What . . . is . . . your . . . name?" he asked slowly, pronouncing each word with difficulty.

"My name is Ben Purcell, lieutenant colonel, U.S. Army."

"What . . . is . . . your . . . name?" he asked again in the same stumbling manner as before.

I had just answered him. I repeated, "My name is Ben Purcell, lieutenant colonel, U.S. Army." When I looked at him, I saw that he was puzzled by my response. He was holding a book and had asked me the question by reading it from the book. Apparently he had expected me to repeat "what is your name?" Instead, I answered his question. Now he sounded out the letters of the alphabet—"A . . . B . . . C . . . D"—and then said, "You say." I realized he was making an effort to learn English and was using me as a tutor. After that, each afternoon for about a week Snoopy would unlock my cell and permit me to bask in the sun. For me this was a very welcome change to the steady routine of being locked up in a small bare cell.

In September 1971 I watched as a mouse entered my cell and scurried around for several minutes before leaving. When the mouse showed up again the following night I decided to set a trap for him with the lid of my toilet bucket. I propped up one side of the lid with a three-inch stick of bamboo to which I had tied a long string raveled from a scrap of cloth. I lay in wait for thirty minutes or so the third night until the mouse showed up again. When he ran under the lid I pulled the string, the lid fell as planned, and I had the mouse.

I spread my extra undershirt on the floor and slowly slid the toilet lid over it, pulled the corners up tightly, turned it over, felt the mouse, and smothered it. Now the question arose as to what I should do with it. I decided to place the now dead mouse on the ledge of the inspection hole in the door to my cell, knowing full well that sometime during the night Snoopy would jerk the sliding panel open and stick his face in the inspection hole.

I did not remain awake that night to see his reaction but I can well imagine the surprised look on his face as he looked squarely at the mouse. Anyway, the mouse was gone the next morning and Snoopy never said a word about it. Perhaps I should have been more considerate of him. Ha!

In November of 1971 Snoopy came by my cell and in broken but understandable English said, "Tomorrow I go away."

"Where?"

Snoopy refused to answer my question, but we did continue our conversation, such as it was. As we talked Snoopy noticed I was having difficulty breathing as a result of my annual bout with sinusitis. After he determined that I was indeed ill he went somewhere (I presume to the first-aid station) and came back with six large pills for me. He then sent a trustee prisoner to a supply room for a package of small bamboo slivers which I used as toothpicks to remove the food which impacted in the large gaps between my deteriorating teeth. As he handed me the bamboo slivers he said, "Good-bye."

Whenever I reflect back on the relationship between Snoopy and me, I see a full range of emotions. First there was the business-as-expected, then the tension resulting from the incident of my comb, followed by the hatred Snoopy must have felt toward me when I escaped. After a brief but rough encounter upon his return in July of 1970, Snoopy returned to the more business-as-expected course and then moved on to a casual friendship as he used me to help develop his skills in English. Finally, Snoopy demonstrated genuine concern for my physical well-being before we parted ways forever.

Had I fallen victim to the Stockholm syndrome, whereby prisoners or hostages develop psychologically distorted friendly feelings toward their captors?

I have thought about this and don't believe that was the case. What I do believe is that normal human beings are inca-

pable of harsh and brutal treatment toward other human beings over extended periods of time. I believe I simply learned
to be patient enough and human enough to allow the best
nature of the guards to come to the surface.

There was also a guard at K-77 who proved to be a friend
on several occasions. His name was On'. (Though he didn't
realize it, On' was the guard who provided me with the essen-
tial information I had needed to plan my escape back in December 1969. It was On' who, in telling me he was going to
a movie in Hanoi, gave me the direction of the city and how
far it was from the camp.)

On' had appeared on the scene one week after my arrival
at K-77 in July of 1968. At first he was cautiously curious.
Mostly he would only slow down as he passed my cell and
take a quick peek inside. It wasn't too long though before he
began stopping for several minutes at a time to try and make
conversation. What an exercise in futility that was!

I was very frustrated at not being able to communicate
with a human being other than an interrogator. At that time
I had had almost four months of isolation and loneliness, and
I yearned for someone I could converse with on an equal
footing. I remember thinking that if only there existed a recognized and accepted international language, we humans
would be a giant step closer to world peace and understanding. With all the scientific advances in other fields, why can't
human beings learn to communicate directly with one another
without having to go through an interpreter? Issues and ideas
lose much of their clarity and meaning when one person can't
communicate directly with another.

Eventually, by using the few words of French we could
both understand, an abundance of sign language, and pointing, we started to understand a few words of the other person's language. Very primitive methods to be sure, but before
many days passed I could count to ten and ask for a few basic
needs such as water, food, medicine, shaves, haircuts, toothpicks, and even tweezers.

It may sound strange that I would ask for tweezers, but
they were necessary. In 1955 I had had surgery to remove a
growth on my lower left eyelid. As a result of that surgery I

had an eyelash which persisted in growing inward toward my eyeball. Prior to my capture I could take care of the problem at home with a mirror, a pair of tweezers and a strong light, with only occasional visits to Dr. John Ball, my optometrist friend.

The eyelash didn't quit growing when I was captured. In fact a new one would grow every three to four weeks. For days the stub would irritate my eyeball until it grew long enough to see with a naked eye and finally get hold of with the crude tweezers I could borrow from On'.

On' had the tweezers because he never shaved. He simply pulled each whisker out by its root as soon as it appeared. He would stand around for hours at a time feeling for hairs and then pluck them out. I used to wonder how he could stand the sting.

There was a fruit tree growing in the prison compound, and when On' was on duty while the other prison cadre were on the two-hour period of rest beginning at noon each day, he would lay his rifle on the ground and climb the tree to pick a few pieces of the fruit, which he always shared with me. The fruit was much like a pear in texture and taste, but the outer surface was a thin, tough layer of green skin resembling a lime. I never found out what kind of fruit it was. On' called it "globe fruit."

Once I concealed a piece of the fruit under my blanket to eat later, but On' became concerned that a *cambo* (his word for turnkey) would smell the fruit during an inspection and realize some guard had violated standing orders not to associate with or befriend an American prisoner. To satisfy On' I immediately ate the fruit in his presence.

In the early spring of 1969 On' brought a thin strip of metal about one-half inch wide and four inches long to my cell. He claimed it was from a downed American aircraft, and he wanted me to fashion a ring for him.

For several hours I worked on this strip of metal, scraping it on the cement floor in order to bevel the ends so they would overlap smoothly and fit his finger. As a circular mold I used a large steel bolt embedded in concrete at the foot of my cot, which was used for attaching stocks and leg irons to punish troublesome prisoners. I even went to the trouble of engraving a few simple designs on the ring, using a small nail which he provided for me. On' was pleased, and I was gratified to have something to do with my hands for a while. It was a moment rich in ironies.

On' told me early in our friendship that he lived in Hanoi and had a wife. Every few months he would tell me that he had been to Hanoi to visit his family. Following those visits he would give me a piece of candy and spend a few minutes conversing with me about his children. I thought of Anne and our children constantly but to have a friend—as On' was now—talk about his recent visits home nearly tore my heart out. I tried not to be envious of his opportunities to see his family, but to be made more keenly aware that I couldn't do the same hurt deeply. I suspected On' sensed my pain and tried to comfort me in the only way he knew how, with the candy and a smile.

Once On' lent me his fountain pen so that I could actually write a letter to Anne. I carefully composed a very brief note, giving only enough personal data and details to insure that should Anne receive the note she would recognize that it was written by me. I then made an envelope from white toilet paper and addressed it to a friend in Paris: "Dr. Henri Vincent, Pasteur, Eglise Baptiste, Rue De Lille, Paris."

I knew that Dr. Vincent, if he received the letter, would be smart enough to share it with our friend Reverend Jack Hancox, a Southern Baptist missionary to France. Jack would then know how to get in touch with Anne. Regardless of how farfetched the idea may have been, it at least provided some ray of hope that my family might know that I was alive.

On' demonstrated a great deal of compassion and friendship as he undertook to help me write the letter and then mail it. He told me later that the postage was seven *hau,* a very small amount in American currency, I'm sure, but for On' a sizeable chunk of his 100-*hau* monthly salary.

He did something else for me that put him at considerable risk. Back in 1968, just after coming to K-77, I was leaving my cell to take a bath one morning when quite by accident of timing another American POW was being let out of his cell at the opposite end of the long cell block. I recognized the American as Captain Ted Gostas, the officer who had been on the truck with me as we traveled north on the Ho Chi Minh Trail and who had walked with me as we departed Bao Cao. Ted didn't see me, but I saw that his prison jacket bore the number 61.

In the spring of 1971 I drew a crude sketch of a prisoner and placed the number 61 on his jacket. I asked On' if he knew where number 61 was now. On' took the sketch, smiled broadly, and departed.

For thirty minutes I was sitting on pins and needles. Would he take the note to Crisco? Would he simply destroy the note and forget my effort to learn about Ted? Or would he, moved by a feeling of friendship, deliver the note to Ted? After waiting for what seemed like hours, although it actually could have been no more than thirty minutes, On' returned. He handed me a note signed by someone who claimed to be Don Rander, an American POW. Don wrote that Captain Ted Gostas and a civilian named Charles Willis were with him in a cell in another section of K-77. In his response Don wrote that he had intercepted my note and did not let Ted know about it for fear that he would inform the authorities.

I was overjoyed at the prospect of communicating with another American if only through the written word. That joy was tempered by the fear that the response could have been written by Crisco as a trick. But how was I to be certain one way or the other?

I composed a second note asking for more information, naively assuming that if I did not sign my own name, Crisco would not be able to prove who the American was that was trying to break camp regulations by contacting other prisoners. After another anxious thirty minutes of waiting, On' returned with another response. This note contained the names of fourteen other prisoners, twelve Americans and two Filipinos, who had been transferred out of K-77 in June of 1971.

I was elated as I composed a third note to Don, my newfound pen-pal. This time I identified myself as Lieutenant Colonel Ben Purcell and did so with complete confidence that On' wouldn't betray me. The new-found opportunity to communicate with other Americans was wonderful and quite unexpected, and I made a decision not to exercise the privilege too often. I decided to wait at least two weeks before making another effort to contact Don.

A few days later I realized On' had not been on duty. I looked for him every day for weeks, but he never showed up again. I have no idea what happened to him. I don't know whether his tour of duty as a prison guard was completed or if he was suspended for befriending an American criminal or whether he was transferred to the battlefront.

For now I can only hope that he survived the war. Someday I would like to meet him under a different set of circumstances. I would also like him to meet my wife and our children.

If I could just get a message to him . . .

19

TRANSFER TO K-49

BEN'S STORY

After lunch one day in mid-December 1971 a guard entered my cell and told me to roll up my clothes in my blanket and prepare to move. He then placed a blindfold over my eyes and led me through the courtyard to a vehicle similar in size to an American jeep. Although I could only peek under the blindfold I was able to determine that there were two metal cages in the rear of the vehicle. One of the cages was already occupied by another prisoner and I was locked into the other cage. Since we could not communicate with each other I didn't learn until weeks later that the other prisoner's name was Gene Weaver.

I wasn't exactly certain where we went but my best estimate was someplace in the mountains about fifty miles north of Hanoi, perhaps in the area of Thai Nguyen. I called the new prison K-49.

When we left K-77 I was absolutely convinced that the war had ended and that I was being taken to Gia Lam airport near Hanoi for release and a flight back home. You can imagine my disappointment when that ever-present hope suffered one more setback.

In many ways K-49 was an improvement over my old situation. My cell was ten feet square, and I had a wooden bed with a four-inch-thick straw mattress. That was the first mattress I had enjoyed since leaving my quarters in Da Nang!

I also had a table and stool which would have been wonderful for writing letters, if they had only let me write letters. It was good, however, for playing solitaire and bridge with my homemade deck of cards.

And how is this for being "uptown"? I had my own private bath complete with toilet, shower, and reservoir of creek water. Of course, the shower was no more than a rubber bucket which I used to dip water from the reservoir and then pour it over my body. The toilet was a block of concrete three feet square and three feet high with a hole in the top. There were two steps in front so I could climb on top. The rubber bucket also served as the vessel by which I was able to flush the toilet. Considering what I had before, though, this was a spectacular improvement.

There were a total of nine cells at K-49, five in one building and four in another. One of the cells in the latter building was twice as large as the other eight. I believed there were two Americans living together in that larger cell because sometimes, when the wind was blowing in the right direction, I could hear Americans conversing.

Each cell had a cage out front. The cage was a high, solid wall of concrete, with barbed wire interlaced across the top. The best thing about the cage was that I was permitted outside each day for fresh air and sunshine. Though our voices would carry over the walls I was still unable to talk to any of the other prisoners, because the guards normally alternated the times that each prisoner was allowed access to his particular cage.

Each morning the guards would open the steel door to my cell and let me out into my cage. It was wonderful to be outside, to be able to look up and see the sky, even if the area was totally enclosed by a concrete wall and covered with barbed wire. After lunch I would remain locked in my cell while the prisoners in the cells on either side of mine had access to their cages. There were three times each day, when the meals were served, that all prisoners had access to their cages at the same time for about fifteen to twenty minutes each.

There was one bad thing about this new prison that caused me a great deal of anxiety. It was a very small prison administered by the civil government, not by the military. Although Crisco escorted me to the new camp, the guards there wore the same type of tan uniform as the policemen at the precinct police station in Hanoi, not the typical green military uniforms worn by the guards at Bao Cao and K-77. For the first time since my capture I believed that I had been placed under civilian control.

I couldn't help but think of all the times they threatened to keep me beyond any truce, and bringing me here would seem to add credence to their threats. After all it was such a small facility that it would be very easy to conceal from aerial observation. It was so new that the cement and mortar were still wet and soft in some places, so it wasn't likely to be on any of our intelligence maps.

Shortly after I arrived at K-49 I made covert contact with another American prisoner! His name was Gene Weaver, and he was in the cell next to mine. Gene was captured in the city of Hue during the Tet offensive in 1968, so we had been prisoners for the same length of time.

Gene and I discovered a drain hole that connected our cages and were able to exchange notes with each other by writing on toilet paper and shoving it through the hole at mealtimes.

At first, I used ink made from soot taken from the lamp and mixed with water. Although that might sound haphazard, it is amazing how black and legible such ink is. It's as good as India ink. Later on, however, I was able to "liberate" a short pencil at the camp headquarters during one of my interrogations.

After swapping personal data to identify ourselves to each other, Gene and I set out to develop a tap code, a system whereby we could send messages to each other at any time, day or night, by tapping on the wall that separated our cells.

Gene had been a B-17 bomber pilot during World War

II and could still remember about half of the Morse Code. This knowledge formed the core of our code, which we built on by designating a pattern of dots and dashes for each missing letter. Gene suggested that a short pause between each tap could represent a dot, while a longer pause would be a dash. I wasn't sure I could distinguish between a longer pause for a dash, a still longer pause for the end of the word, and a longer pause still for the end of a sentence.

After several days of debating the issue I suggested that two rapid taps in succession would represent a dash, and Gene accepted the idea.

Each day, just after our noon meal, we "opened the net" and exchanged a few words using a unique code that only two people in the whole world knew. We'd record each transmitted letter on the bottom of our metal drinking cups so when we ended the conversation a quick swipe with a moist thumb destroyed all evidence. After several weeks of practice we could send and receive about four or five words per minute.

In one of our earliest notes Gene stated that he, too, was worried about the fact that K-49 was a state prison as opposed to a military installation. He was particularly worried, he confided to me, because he wasn't military at all—he was CIA. The interrogators knew that he was a member of the CIA, he told me.

As you can imagine, that gave me increased cause for worry because the Vietnamese still insisted that I was CIA. I wondered if that meant we were to be treated differently from the other prisoners.

Actually, I was already being treated differently. I had been a prisoner for four years and I had been kept in solitary confinement for almost the entire time: forty-eight long and depressing months with no one to talk to and no word from home. I had no indication that anyone in America knew I was alive.

To keep my sanity during that period I managed to develop a routine of mental and physical exercises which had to be performed daily and on a precise schedule. Whenever I was taken out of my cell for interrogations my schedule would be thrown off, but I would force myself to work on into the night to complete that particular day's self-imposed work assignment.

It isn't possible to say what I missed most. There were times I missed good food more than anything else. At other times I would have an intense desire to be with Anne and to share our love. I also missed the opportunity to work with my hands and to participate in sporting events such as bowling or softball. But one thing I missed all the time was conversation. I wanted to be sitting in our living room talking with Anne, with the kids, and with our friends. It wouldn't matter what we were talking about, for just the act of conversation would have been enough to satisfy me. At least now I had established some contact and was exchanging covert messages with another American, but how I missed talking with my loved ones.

From the moment I arrived at K-49 I was determined to try another escape.

I didn't even have to talk myself into trying. The only question on my mind was when I would go. It didn't take me ten minutes to realize that I could get out through the barbed wire that covered the cage anytime I wanted to. I started getting myself ready for the attempt.

The first time I had escaped I had had to drill and cut my way through the wooden door. I didn't need to do that this time, and it was a good thing because this door was made of steel. Although the logistics of this escape would be different, there were, nevertheless, things to be done. The preparation would be just as tedious and involved.

The way I saw it there would be four problems.

Problem number one would be in buying enough time to get away from the vicinity of the prison before I was missed. The guards were on constant patrol during the daytime and were always looking into my cage through an inspection port while I was outside during the morning hours. It was approximately thirty minutes between their inspection tours. If I could fool them into thinking I was there for just one turn, it would buy me an hour. I estimated that in one hour I could climb through the barbed wire covering the cage, crawl under the perimeter fence, and still have enough time to run into the nearby woods.

However, if I escaped in the morning while I had access

to the cage the guards would have several hours of daylight to search for me. I decided I needed to escape during the evening meal, when I would have access to the cage for a few minutes but it would soon be dark.

Problem number two would be in finding my direction once I was outside the prison. I remembered the frustration of being lost during my first attempt. I was so disoriented that I was still wandering around the next morning, and that was my downfall.

Problem number three was to make certain I was in good enough physical condition to survive the ordeal.

And problem number four was having a destination where I could reasonably expect to be rescued. Since I had headed for the French consulate the first time I escaped, I would have to come up with a different destination this time. I figured that the moment my absence was discovered, they would probably put someone outside the Consulate of the Republic of France.

The rest of the world may have had no idea where I was, or even that I existed, but here in North Vietnam I was notorious.

20

ESCAPE FROM K-49

BEN'S STORY

I worked on my escape plan night and day and finally came up with an answer to all four problems.

For my destination I decided to head for the coast, borrow a fishing boat, and row out to sea. The prevailing ocean current off shore would cause my boat to drift southward, toward where the bulk of the U.S. Navy was deployed. That may sound like a far-fetched idea, but it wasn't farfetched at all. I knew that the U.S. Air Force and the U.S. Navy controlled the skies and the seas all around Vietnam. They were on constant patrol, and nothing moved in the air or on the surface of the ocean without their knowledge. If I suddenly showed up in a small boat they'd have someone investigating me within minutes. The next step would be for them to send a helicopter out to pick me up and ferry me back to the ship, and I'd be on my way home. If that was simplistic, then its simplicity was its beauty.

I addressed the physical conditioning requirement of my plan by exercising on a daily basis. I started out by running in place at a very strenuous pace, but before long I began having severe chest twinges that made me dizzy. I was afraid the twinges might be a signal from my heart that I was over-exerting. I didn't want to get out of the prison only to drop dead of a heart attack somewhere in the jungle. I quit running in place so hard and toned down my other exercises to a more sedate level. I paced back and forth in my cell barefooted to toughen up my feet while gaining endurance. I remembered what it was like when I was first captured, how I suffered so with my blistered feet. I didn't intend to let that happen again.

I also addressed the problem of getting lost. Part of my difficulty my first time out was that I was unsure of my cardinal directions. I believed that had I known with any degree of certainty which way was north, I might have made good my escape. I solved that for my second attempt.

One day quite by accident I chipped off a corner of one of the razor blades while I was shaving. As I looked at the chipped piece of metal, I remembered that as a child I had successfully floated a needle on water. I wondered if I could float this razor-blade chip. To my surprise the chip did float and it pointed about ten degrees east of north. When I turned it over to the other side it pointed about ten degrees west of north.

Reflecting back to my days as a physics major at North Georgia College in Dahlonega, I realized that the metal chip was magnetic but the lines of force ran through it at an angle. To determine magnetic north I had to find a way to get the metal sliver to stand on its edge so that this angle would not be significant.

I put the metal sliver upright on a tiny piece of soap and floated the soap on a scrap of paper in a bowl of water. The magnetized piece of razor blade swung around to the general direction of north. In order to make this discovery useful on the trail, I experimented further by using a piece of string, unraveled from my socks, to suspend the razor chip in mid-air. Slowly but surely the homemade compass needle came around to point toward north.

I had just reinvented the compass! With this device, primitive though it was, I felt I would be able to navigate my way eastward to the Tonkin Gulf.

The most difficult task, it seemed to me, would be to

secure the extra time I would need between the guard's rounds. I thought about making a dummy and putting him in bed as I did at K-77 in December of 1969. I even started playing with ideas for fashioning the head.

But that wasn't sure enough. If the guard was the least bit suspicious, or if he thought I might be ill and enter my cell to check on me, he would discover I was gone. I kept trying to think of other ways to buy the extra time and kept coming back to the idea of a dummy, but I knew a regular dummy wasn't the answer—unless there was some way for the dummy to talk to the guard. And of course that wasn't possible.

But, I thought, what if I had the dummy interact with the guard in some other way—do something to convince the guard that it was a real person? As soon as I thought of that, I knew I had a possible solution but also another problem. The challenge was, how could I make the dummy interact with the guard?

Then I hit upon an idea. It involved placing a dummy on the toilet in the rear of my cell.

The bathroom was actually a little room separated by a doorway from the cell proper but visible from the cell door. If I happened to be standing on the platform in the toilet to urinate, the guard at the cell door could see me only from the shoulders down.

I remembered that a few weeks earlier I had been urinating when the guard came around for the evening check and to pick up the supper dishes. He looked in, saw me in the bathroom, and heard the sound of water splashing but didn't come into the bathroom to check my presence physically.

I made a point to do that again . . . and again the guard, satisfied with what he saw and heard, didn't come back to the toilet to check on me.

After that I made a habit of being in the bathroom urinating at exactly the time he came by to pick up the supper dishes and to make his final check for the day. I even began slowly pouring a cup of water into the toilet to add to the sound effects, and the guard, perfectly satisfied with what he was seeing and hearing, never checked more carefully. For several weeks I conditioned all the guards to expect to find me on the toilet on their final check for the day.

Now I knew how to make my dummy, a perfectly fascinating fellow I called Charlie, interact with the guard.

I made Charlie by filling my rubber bucket with water and then suspending it over the toilet with excess cord from my mosquito net. Across the top of the bucket I placed a wide piece of bamboo from which I hung the blouse of my spare prison uniform. With a little artistic draping here and there I was able to make the blouse assume the fullness of a man's upper body.

I folded my trousers in half so as not to impede the flow of water and stitched them to the lower back of the blouse. I used a homemade bone needle and thread from unraveled scraps of cloth. I put thin bamboo strips in the trouser cuffs to round the legs out and make them appear more realistic. Then I stood at the front door and glanced toward the bathroom. I was convinced that the dummy looked very much like a man standing on a three-foot-high toilet. The fact that Charlie had no head didn't matter because the guard couldn't see the head from the front door anyway.

What Charlie did have was even more important than a head. He had a way to interact with the guard, because he had a bladder.

I punched a hole in the bottom of the rubber bucket, plugged the hole, then filled the bucket with water. When I pulled the plug from the bucket, a thin stream of water began pouring down into the toilet in an exact duplication of the sound made by a man urinating.

My best estimate was that Charlie would "go" for about twenty-five minutes. Since I had been standing in the toilet at the same time for two weeks running and since none of the guards had come in to check on me personally, they would see exactly what they expected to see and hear exactly what they had already heard several times before.

Although all the problems seemed to have an answer now, I was still concerned about my health. After exercising strenuously following the evening meal on the seventeenth of

March, I squatted down with my back against the wall and tried to make a decision whether to go or not to go.

During those moments I had a mental conversation with my son Cliff. In my fantasy I had gotten back home and was telling him of my planned second escape. I told him I had been confident I could get out of the prison but had not been quite sure I would make it back home because of my health. Cliff looked at me with a question in his eyes and said, "But why didn't you try, Dad? Why didn't you try?"

I was convinced that I would have to try or I could never face Cliff again.

In the spring of 1970 at K–77 I had fashioned a pair of walking shorts, complete with pockets, from scrap cloth. I decided to wear them on this escape so I would have them as a memento once I got home. And from the material I had left over I made another cap. I also made another small replica of the U.S. flag and an identification card. I wrapped each of these tightly in cellophane taken from a cigarette package and stitched each in the upper corner of one of the pockets in the handmade shorts. My clothes probably wouldn't have stood the test of close scrutiny, but then neither would my white face. From a distance, though, I might not stand out as being too different from a Vietnamese cadreman.

It was March 18, 1972, and I was ready to go. The turnkey delivered the evening meal of squash and rice. I drank the juice off the squash and placed the remainder of the meal in a used plastic sugar bag to eat later on the trail. I unfastened several ties that held the barbed wire in place just above the cell door; then I went back to the toilet, pulled the plug from Charlie, and remained just long enough to make sure he was "doing his thing." Now I estimated that I had approximately twenty-five minutes to get out of the cell and hide until it became dark enough to travel with some degree of safety. If I was lucky I would have the entire night to put distance between me and the prison compound.

I prayed that I would be kept safe and be given the courage to see the effort through.

The first part went exactly as planned. I quickly climbed the metal cell door, moved the barbed wire aside, and went through the top of my cage. I knew that this

was the most dangerous moment of the entire escape, for
if a guard happened to be in the tower near camp headquarters he would have a clear shot at me as I went up
through the barbed wire.

My prayer was answered, for the guard had apparently
gone to supper, leaving the tower unattended. I replaced
the barbed wire in its original position and crawled along
a board that passed over the cages but underneath the
eaves of the building. The board was used to hold the
strands of barbed wire that ran at right angles to the building. As I passed over his cage, I saw Gene Weaver in
person for the first time. We exchanged hellos and he gave
me the V sign for victory.

I continued along the board until I got to the end of
the cell block, dropped off the eight-foot-high wall surrounding the cages, slipped under the exterior bamboo security fence by way of a drainage ditch, and headed for
the woods. I soon found myself in a small stream, listening
to the frogs sing as I ran away from the prison, bent over
to better avoid detection.

I figured I would have at least twenty more minutes until
they missed me, so I intended to get as far away during that
time as I could. As I ran my feet made little splashing sounds
and my breath came in gasps. I recalled the chest pains I had
experienced during my exercise periods, so I forced myself to
slow down to conserve energy.

Around me the night was getting dark and the air was
filled with the sounds of freedom—frogs, crickets, a dog barking somewhere in the distance . . . and no prison walls!

When I had traveled a little over an hour I began to see
lights moving around in a nearby hamlet. My first thought was
that they had discovered my absence and were searching for
me, so I went around the hamlet and continued to move
through the night, making certain that I did nothing to give
myself away.

It wasn't long until a farmer's dog sensed some stranger
was nearby and began to bark. I was close to a picket fence
that surrounded the farmer's yard, so I just squatted down
and froze in place. The dog kept barking. Soon the farmer
came out of his cabin carrying a firebrand. He walked to

within twenty feet of me, his dog barking louder all the time. Since he could neither see nor hear anything that would cause the barking, the farmer spoke harshly to his dog to quiet it; then he returned to his house. A few minutes later I slipped away as quietly as I could.

A problem occurred with the compass. The night was so dark that I was absolutely unable to see it let alone determine the direction in which it pointed. But I could make out the shape of a mountain in the distance so I traveled in that direction. I started climbing the mountain in order to get a better look at my surroundings and to be ready to move out toward the coast after a day of rest.

By dawn I had made it to the top of the mountain, where I found a thicket of bushes under which to hide. I spent the entire day there, resting, hoping an American plane would fly over. I had a small piece of glass which I could use to signal the pilot. Perhaps I could be picked up without having to go to the coast.

No aircraft passed for the entire day. (Years later I learned that in mid-March of 1972 our forces were observing a temporary halt in the bombing of North Vietnam.)

Late in the afternoon a woodcutter began chopping down a large tree nearby. He cut a notch in the side of the tree facing me, and I realized he planned to have the tree fall right on the bushes where I was hiding!

What should I do? I certainly didn't want to get hit by a falling tree after going to so much trouble to get where I was. I decided to leave my hiding place. The woodcutter was a bit surprised to see me, but he kept cutting the tree down. I simply moved to another hiding place about five hundred yards away and waited for darkness.

Although the day was fraught with danger, it was nevertheless a day of freedom. I lay out in that patch of woods, feeling the air, listening to the birds, looking up at the blue sky through the green leaves, and rejoicing in the sensation of liberty.

When the sun set that night I felt elated. I had been out for more than twenty-four hours, longer than during my first attempt. I had successfully eluded recapture all day long. Now, with darkness, I would be able to move again without being seen. I wasn't certain how far it was to the coast, but thanks to my compass I at least knew which way to go. Maybe I could make it before morning. If not, I thought, I would merely find a place to spend the day and go on the next night. I was prepared to go on for as many days and nights as it took. I was full of confidence and hope.

After the sun went down I came down the eastern side of the mountain to continue my journey. I headed for the nearest stream to get a drink of water, passing very near to several people in the process. Once a man came so close to me I could have reached out and hit him with the stick I was carrying. I hid under a hedge when I heard him approaching. He turned off the road and onto a path leading up to his house. The hedge, which was my hiding place, separated the path from a nearby garden.

Before long I found the stream and quenched my thirst. I was totally dehydrated by now from a combination of my poor physical condition, the excitement of the escape, and the lack of any food or water during the preceding twenty-four hours. Like a good infantryman, I also changed my socks and rinsed out the pair I had been wearing.

As I sat on a large rock in the middle of the rapidly flowing mountain stream, I noticed a strange beam of light that appeared to be shooting out in many different directions. As the light came closer I could hear the engine of a vehicle, and I realized that it had to be a search party looking for me. The light was a spotlight playing its beam all around. I looked around for a place to hide.

The first place I found was in a large hollow tree. After the vehicle passed, I began to move again and almost immediately came face to face with a water buffalo that was tied to a fence post. The poor animal was very frightened, and it began snorting and trying to break away. I was frightened, too, but I had the good judgment to keep quiet and move out of its way.

I continued to move on and a bit later came to within twenty feet of a member of another search party. He didn't see me because I was wearing black pajamas, whereas he was wearing white ones. When he turned his back toward me I did a low crab crawl to my right and got behind a nearby bush until he left the area. I don't know if I became careless from overconfidence after that or if it was just a freak accident, but sometime later I suddenly walked right into an armed patrol. They weren't showing flashlights and they weren't talking, so I had no warning that they were in front of me. The real irony is that they were as surprised to see me as I was to see them. I could have avoided them if only I had known they were there.

Although my sudden presence may have surprised them, they were obviously aware of who I was because they recovered very quickly. Half a dozen of them aimed their weapons at me and I heard the terribly disturbing metallic crash of rounds being chambered. All it would take now would be for one nervous North Vietnamese soldier to touch his trigger, and I would be killed.

With a resigned sigh I stood very still. The soldiers quickly tied my hands together behind my back, and we started walking back toward the prison.

It had become my custom at K-49 to whistle a few tunes each Sunday evening before going to bed. I'd always begin with a familiar Stephen Foster song, such as "My Old Kentucky Home," followed by a favorite hymn such as "Whispering Hope." I would then whistle the songs of the four military services and end it all with the "Star Spangled Banner."

On the trip back to K-49 I remembered it was Sunday, March 19, 1972, so I started my customary Sunday whistling concert. The guards were so happy to have recaptured me that they did not seem to mind at all and even smiled broadly as I ended my songs with the "Star Spangled Banner." I wondered if they really knew that I was whistling my National Anthem.

Within an hour I was back at K-49 facing an irate camp director. There must have been fifty soldiers standing around in the courtyard. Evidently my escape had set in motion a massive manhunt requiring a considerable expenditure of manpower. I was very weak from the lack of food and water plus my energy expenditure during the last thirty hours, so when the camp director had me blindfolded and used me as a punching bag, I couldn't stay on my feet.

Before long I was taken back to my cell, where I saw

that my table, stool, and straw mattress had been thrown out into the cage. I was pushed back into the cell amid the shouts and curses of the guards. I expected to be put in stocks again, but that didn't happen. It didn't matter. I was so despondent over my failure this time that nothing they could do to me would have made my mood any worse.

As soon as the guards left my cell I heard the now familiar sound of Gene tapping a message to me.

"How is your health?"

I tapped back, "Okay."

It was wonderful to know that another American was nearby and that he cared for my health.

Without the straw mattress I had become used to, the wooden bed was very uncomfortable. But in spite of this discomfort, and even though I was bothered by thirst and hunger, I soon dropped off into a deep sleep brought on by sheer exhaustion.

The next day I had a surprise. Crisco suddenly showed up at my cell. I hadn't seen Crisco since he escorted me to K-49 back in December. Along with Crisco were several military guards. The state security guards had been removed, to be replaced by soldiers wearing military uniforms, with military rank.

"Are you surprised to see me again?" Crisco asked.

"Yes," I admitted.

"Civilians," Crisco said, spitting in disdain as he watched the civil guards getting ready to leave. "They have no business here."

"I must say that I am glad to see the military back," I said.

"Why is that?"

I didn't want to tell him that I was afraid that if the civilians stayed on here we might never get back home.

"I am a professional soldier," I answered. "If I am to be a prisoner of war I prefer to be the prisoner of soldiers."

"Yes," Crisco said. "I can understand that." Crisco looked at me for a long moment. "I am very disappointed in you, Purcell. You have behaved very badly once again."

Crisco turned and walked away from the cell, but I thought I saw the glimmer of respect in his eyes. Then I suddenly realized something. Crisco had called me by name. That was the first time in almost five years I had heard my name spoken.

The next day I was brought before the camp director for punishment. He declared that I would receive only one-half of my ration of food for thirty days and would not be allowed out in the cage for a like period. I was surprised that the punishment was not more severe.

Later that same day I received a tapped message from Gene.

"Good job, Ben. You have blown the security of this prison. I believe they had intended to hold the nine of us back as bargaining chips after the war. Now they can't, thanks to you. Don't be down on yourself. You may have been recaptured, but you did us all a big favor."

That message raised my self-esteem, but I knew I didn't want it to go to my head. I was still a prisoner of war.

And I was still resisting—because another interesting thing had happened as a result of my escape. The military guards decided one guard tower wasn't enough to watch over the entire camp. They built a second tower near my cage and manned it twenty-four hours a day. From the second tower the guard on duty could look down into my cage and observe every move I made. If nothing else, my escape attempt had caused the guard force to be doubled at our camp, and that removed seven soldiers from possible duty on the battlefield.

There was also something else that I got a chuckle out of. When the guards came around to lock me in the cell for the night—it didn't seem to matter where I was standing in the cell—they would pass me and go directly to the rear of the cell and check the toilet thoroughly. Apparently they had received orders to Check Purcell's Toilet, and unwilling to be burned again, they followed those orders to the letter, no matter what.

Because of the increased observation of my activities I decided to play it cool and not try any more escapes, at least not anytime soon. I would have to find some other activity to occupy my hands and mind such as sewing and making small objects of interest.

During the first two or three years the guards were very strict about not letting me make anything without their permission, which they would never grant as a matter of policy. Even so I succeeded in making three rings and a pair of shorts, as well as a map case and fatigue hat for my first escape. Now, following my second escape, they relaxed their objection to my work on small items, probably thinking it was better for me to be busy working on harmless items than plotting another escape.

21

POEM

One of the things that hurt most after my capture in 1968 was having my wedding band taken from me. On Anne's and my anniversary in 1969 I made a makeshift ring from my toothbrush handle, but after several months it crumbled. As a replacement I made a ring from the aluminum contained in a toothpaste tube. (We were issued one tube every ninety days, and I saved all the empties.) I was wearing that ring when I escaped in December 1969, but they took it from me when I was recaptured.

Finally, in January 1970 I made a ring from a strip of bamboo, and because I grew smarter in the way I handled it, I was able to keep it the remainder of the time I was a prisoner of war. As part of my morning ritual I would put the ring on my finger for a few minutes and during those few minutes I would think of Anne and the five children. Somehow Anne seemed closer to me during those few moments of reflection. However, I learned that the ring wasn't safe if I kept it on my finger all the time, so after a few minutes I would slip it off, tie it to the drawstring of my undershorts, and drop it down inside. They never strip-searched me, so I succeeded in safeguarding the ring until I was released. How I looked forward to the day I could trade the bamboo ring for one of gold that I would have Anne place on my finger.

One of the advantages of my escapes was the therapeutic value of the work involved, not only in the planning and execution but also in making the necessary tools. I put that same craftsmanship to work by making artifacts to help pass the time.

I made quite a few things, but the one I was most proud of was my communion set. It consisted of a chalice, a plate, and a cover with a cross. It was beautiful. I did more than just look at it, though. On the first Sunday of every month I would wash my handkerchief so I could use it as a fair cloth; then with a crust of bread or a few grains of rice and a few drops of water I would celebrate communion.

During those moments I would think of all the communions Anne and I had celebrated together, and I would sense her presence. But there was a bittersweetness to it because even though I felt her spiritual proximity I missed her physically and it was hard for me to accommodate. At such times, though, I would look at the cross and tell myself, "Ben, there is someone who has suffered a lot more than you'll ever have to suffer."

In times past, church attendance and the outward appearance of religion were very important to me. Everything became more real to me now. When I thought of the risen Lord I wasn't merely thinking of an abstract concept, I was thinking of a fact. I felt the Lord's presence there with me . . . really felt it as I had never felt it before. At such times I could actually believe that the entire episode wasn't an ordeal but a gift from God. He had given me the rare privilege of sharing him in a way that most can never experience.

That is why I made the communion set in May 1972. This is *how* I made it.

I had learned that the aluminum from the toothpaste tubes made marvelous construction material, and since I never threw away the empty tubes I had quite a bit of the aluminum on hand.

At first I tried to shape the plate and its cover by hand,

mashing it with my fingers. It looked all right, I suppose, but it didn't have the smooth finished look that I really wanted. I considered the problem for a few days and then found a solution. In order to make a finished product I would need a mold of some sort. So my first step was to fashion one.

I hit upon the idea of using toilet paper and rice. By using the rice as a bonding agent and applying it to the rough, brown paper they gave us for toilet paper (initially we received one sheet about ten by twelve inches per week), I was able to come up with a pasteboard material of considerable strength. This was the raw material for the mold. Next I had to shape it.

Prisoners received a razor once every two or three weeks. On one of those occasions all I had to do was cut a few circles out of the pasteboard I had concocted and then shape the circles into doughnutlike molds. (Of course, I did the cutting after I had used the blade for shaving.) That done, I pressed the aluminum tubing into the molds, and out came the communion plate and cover.

The cup was made by putting the ends of two toothpaste tubes together. Next I melted some plastic taken from an empty container of medicine similar to mentholatum and poured it in the hole to hold the two pieces together and to make it waterproof.

I also made a cigarette holder. Although I didn't smoke, I requested the daily ration of six cigarettes so that I could throw them over the cage wall to adjacent prisoners. I made the holder just for something to do. I made salt and pepper shakers, too, but because I had escaped, they didn't allow me to keep salt or pepper in my cell. If they ever had allowed it, though, I would have been prepared.

I also became a tailor. The pair of shorts which I wore on my second escape were made earlier while I was still in K-77. A pair of prisoner trousers became so badly worn that I tore them off at the knees, opened up the seams, and used the material to fashion a comfortable pair of walking shorts. Again, I used a handmade bone needle and unraveled string for the project.

Those shorts even had pockets, adjustable tabs on the waist band, and a fly in front. I made the buttons for the fly from pieces of bone that I would occasionally get in a bowl of soup. I drilled holes in the buttons using a small drill, similar to the one I made before I escaped the first time.

One large button at my waist had the initials of all the members of my family: A for Anne, D for David, another D for Debbie, C for Clarice, another C for Cliff, S for Sherri, and J for Joy. As when I wore the bamboo wedding band, I felt a sense of closeness to my family when I wore those shorts and saw the button with their initials.

Except for the one fleeting moment when I saw Gene Weaver as I escaped, it had now been four years and two months since I had seen or spoken to another American. In all that time the only American voices I had ever heard were indistinct voices on the wind, occasional cries in the night, or the taped voices of the American prisoners who made propaganda broadcasts for the North Vietnamese. Whether those tapes were made because of torture or because of promises of better treatment I didn't know. But I seriously doubted they were achieving the intended purpose of encouraging American soldiers in South Vietnam to protest the war. I wondered if the tapes were being broadcast in the States. If so, what did the American public think about them? Did they think these men represented all of us who were prisoners here? I hoped not.

Spit once told me that Jane Fonda had come to Hanoi to tell the North Vietnamese that most Americans support them in this war. He told me she was a very famous American actress and that by coming over here she had shown the American government that the American people no longer had the will to fight.

I'm not sure why he told me all of this. I suppose it was like everything else here, a ploy to break my spirit. He was so sure I would be impressed by the appearance of Jane Fonda that I didn't have the heart to tell him that I wasn't even sure who Jane Fonda was. I thought perhaps she might be the daughter of Henry Fonda, the man who played Wyatt Earp in the movie *My Darling Clementine*. But if that was so, I didn't see how she could have much of an impact on anything. People had heard of her father, but they had never heard of her, had they?

Spit didn't realize it, but by telling me about Jane Fonda he had reminded me of *My Darling Clementine,* which got me thinking of a few others. It's amazing, but when you find yourself in total isolation it becomes possible to re-create in your mind practically anything you have ever read, seen, or experienced.

I discovered that power first in reciting passages from the Bible shortly after I was captured when I was able to recall the Twenty-third Psalm. It was in that same vein that I found I could celebrate communion by reciting the exact words from the book of Luke in the New Testament.

I also found that I could re-create any book or movie I had ever seen. Thanks to Spit's reminding me of Henry Fonda, I saw *My Darling Clementine* again just by running the film in my mind. It was a good western and I enjoyed it. This, like the therapeutic value of working on my objets d'art, helped to pass the time.

I thought about my duties with the army and realized I would have a lot of information to share when I returned. I could remember the E & E, or Escape and Evasion, classes I went through or even conducted at Fort Benning. And I remembered with a sense of dark humor the training films about how to behave as a prisoner, especially with regard to keeping faith with your fellow prisoners, establishing the proper chain of command, and so on.

Of course, then all of our classes and training films were based upon the experiences we had had in World War II and Korea. In those wars the prisoners were kept in large camps in barracks buildings. They were able to organize escape committees, entertainment committees, information committees, and so forth. The operative word there was committees.

Committees.

I found it very difficult to be involved in a committee of one.

One.

I was lost in the wilderness . . . on the dark side of the moon . . . on a deserted island . . . at the South Pole.

Robinson Crusoe had his Friday. The man without a country had his shipmates.

I was alone.

Why did the North Vietnamese choose this particular method of torture for us? I'm sure it was us, and not just me, because those indistinct voices I'd sometimes hear on the wind came from only one of the nine cells here at K-49. Therefore, the other eight cells must house only one prisoner each.

Although Crisco and Spit told me that all I had to do was make a tape for them, I never believed them. I believed that if the other Americans had been kept together like the prisoners in World War II and Korea, I would have known it. Even though they closed my door whenever another American was in a cage, I would have known if more than one person had been in the cages nearby.

No. What I believed more likely was that they were kept in cells like mine, although perhaps close enough together that some communication between them was possible. I had to hand it to the Vietnamese, they had chosen a very subtle but most effective form of torture.

News about peace continued to ebb and flow. One week the news we would receive indicated a strong possibility for an early cease-fire, but the next week the news dashed all but the slightest hope. Since all the news was controlled by the Vietnamese, I took it with a grain of salt and tried to read between the lines to find the slightest bit of hope.

Gene Weaver was different. He didn't like to be up one day and down the next. He had decided that he wasn't going to be released for another year at best, and maybe two. Maybe he was a stronger-willed person than I was, but I couldn't see how anyone could live without hope.

For more than four years, even during periods of depression, I had greeted each sunrise as a new day of hope.

"This is the day that peace will come to this war-torn land. This is the day of your freedom, Ben. This is the day you'll be going home."

Then as the sun set that evening and I found myself still in prison I would tell myself that tomorrow would be here soon and tomorrow would bring peace.

When we arrived at K-49 in December 1971 I began to believe that peace was a possibility because of little things I noticed. The guards' attitude toward us seemed to change slightly, and Crisco began to show more concern for our health.

One indicator of this concern was our increased ration of sugar. While at K-77 in January of 1969 we started receiving a spoonful of sugar with a piece of bread for breakfast. Then when we were transferred to K-49, we were given a plastic bag containing almost two pounds of sugar. When I asked a guard, "How long does this bag have to last me?" he replied: "When you use this one up we will give you another one." Not only did I use it on the breakfast bread, but I also liked to put a spoonful on a bowl of rice, heat it over the kerosene lamp, and enjoy a bowl of warm rice pudding after each meal.

While the increase in the sugar ration was great, it did cause a problem. The ants descended on the bag by the thousands. I tried moving it from place to place, even hanging it by a string on my mosquito net. Still the ants found the sugar.

One day Gene wrote me a note complaining, "Those tiny two-tenths-of-a-millimeter ants are in my sugar bag. I can see them on the wall all the way across my cell making a beeline for the bag."

In response I corrected Gene, telling him, "The ants are not two-tenths of a millimeter; they are two millimeters long."

Gene disagreed with my statement and held to his previous estimate. I tried to prove my point by making tiny dots on a piece of toilet paper, but I couldn't make one as small as two-tenths of a millimeter.

By this time Gene was fed up with the argument and strongly suggested that we drop it. He said, "Neither one of us has lost an argument in over four years and we're not about to lose one now!" For over four years we had been arguing with ourselves and always winning. This incident became my first step back toward civilization, as I realized that I must always consider the viewpoints of others.

The ant problem was solved the next day when a guard provided us with a metal plate filled with water. He placed a large rock in the water and put the sugar bag on the rock. It worked. The ants would not cross the water barrier.

At about this same time I tried to establish communication with the American in the cell on the other side of mine. I recognized the voice as being that of Captain Ted Gostas, whom I had met on the Ho Chi Minh Trail back in 1968, the same person who had been tortured at Bao Cao, traveled with me to K-77, and arrived at K-49 the day after I did in December.

After recognizing his voice I tried for several days to contact Ted using the same system that had worked so well with Gene. For some reason Ted was hesitant to respond. Apparently he feared the certain punishment should our communication efforts be discovered.

After the fourth or fifth try Ted did respond but his strange message contained only the words, "Forgive me, forgive me."

"Forgive you for what?" I sent back.

"Forgive me. Forgive me."

After a couple more exchanges of the same type, I sent a tersely worded note to Captain Gostas informing him that I was a lieutenant colonel and he was a captain and that I was giving him a direct order to tell me what I was to forgive him for. His answer stunned me.

"Early, during the interrogations, the Vietnamese asked me what I knew about you. I told them I had seen your photograph on the cover of *Time* magazine and that you were a major general."

I was shocked beyond belief. Why would he do such a thing? My only thought was that Ted had hoped to find favor with his interrogator by providing him with interesting, albeit false, information.

Now I realized that the Vietnamese had some basis for their belief that I wasn't an infantry lieutenant colonel but a member of the CIA.

Despite the improved treatment at K-49, I suffered a real downer on David's nineteenth birthday in October 1972. He had been only thirteen and entering the ninth grade when I left Boonville for Vietnam way back in August of 1967. One of my deepest regrets since that time was in not having spent more time with David and the other children when I had the opportunity. Somewhere in the back of my mind was the notion that mothers raised children until they were teenagers and then dads could step in and take over. Parenting does not and should not work that way. I saw that truth quite clearly on David's birthday.

Trying to ignore the pain of being apart, I spent much of the day developing a list of presents I would give David if only I had the chance. As I paced my cell twenty-six times, I thought of a different gift for each letter of the alphabet. For instance, on the first trip I picked automobile for A. By the time I reached the end of the alphabet, David was loaded down with gifts. As a matter of fact, I had done this for each of the children's birthdays for four years. Over the years Anne and the children had received a barn full of gifts, including a lot of X-ray machines and zebras.

I wondered what David really received on his nineteenth birthday. And I wondered where he was. I knew he should be in college by now. He was always such a good student that I knew he would do well at whatever he set his mind to.

It wouldn't be long before Cliff's birthday, then Joy's birthday, and then Christmas would arrive. How could I ever make up to our children the void they experienced by having only one parent near to hear their problems and share their happy moments? How could I ever make this loss up to Anne? I didn't know how, but I knew I would try.

On November 21, 1972, I spent a lot of time thinking about what had happened to us thirteen years before while we were living in France.

Those were very sad days, but remembering how Anne faced that terrible experience thirteen years before gave me assurance that from that same reservoir of strength she would manage to be a wonderful mother and father to our five remaining children.

As I reflected on that terrible day in our lives, I decided to try to write a poem. I had never done anything like that before. To record my thoughts I used a sheet of notebook paper that Crisco had given me the previous Christmas for the purpose of making a paper chain to decorate my cell. The verses I composed in memory of Clarice may never be classic, but the words and thoughts came straight from my heart.

IN MEMORY OF CLARICE

No lovelier child ever graced a home,
nor purer soul passed into the unknown,

than this precious daughter with eyes so
    bright,
who has taken her place with the stars at
    night.
Her hair was like threads of the finest gold,
her smile so warm it chased the cold.
Her soft, clear voice would often ring,
spreading joy and happiness as she would
    sing.
This brave little girl tho' her suffering was
    severe,
would never complain to those she held
    dear.
Without waiting for mom or dad to lead the
    way,
she passed through the veil and slipped
    quietly away.
Our hearts still grieve, the pain shall never
    pass,
for the loss of "Sissie," our bonnie little lass.
But eternal in our memory is her sweet
    smile,
and that greatest of blessings,
having had her awhile.

        Love,
        Dad
        Somewhere in Vietnam
        November 1972

22

THE SECRET MEETING

ANNE'S STORY

In May of 1972 Major Bangasser, who worked at the Pentagon, flew to Fort Benning and met secretly with me and with Colonel Gluck, who was now my ninth FSAO. The previous eight had been moved to new assignments. Major Bangasser told me that through secret intelligence sources the Department of the Army had learned that Ben had been taken to North Vietnam after his capture. He said he didn't know how Ben was at that time, or even if he was still alive. Because this information was sensitive, the source couldn't be revealed to me, and I was asked not to tell anyone about the message.

I agreed but I did request that Major Bangasser tell our son David. The major flew to New York, rented a car, and drove to West Point, where he met with David and honored my request. All of this information was given to us verbally; nothing was put in writing.

This information didn't change my feelings, but I couldn't help wondering what to make of it. Had Ben done something that brought his situation to the attention of intelligence-gathering sources in North Vietnam? Was he sick, hurt, or even dead? Had he taken part in a demon-stration or escape attempt? I wished I had known the full story.

I was still following my middle-of-the-road attitude, not giving up but at the same time trying to face the fact that Ben might not come home. I had shared these feelings with our children. I felt they needed to be prepared, to whatever extent one can prepare for such a thing. It was difficult to live this way, and I needed some positive reinforcement that he was at least alive.

After my prayer of relinquishment I had been able to establish and maintain some emotional stability. Because I was not receiving letters from Ben, I did not have to cope with the emotions letters might arouse. Had I been receiving mail, I probably would have been looking for clues to his health and welfare as well as to his mental stability. Reading between the lines would have been another frustration. I felt that his being over forty was a plus in terms of his mental and emotional ability to cope with the situation, but I was concerned that Ben's being older would give him more problems physically.

Initially I didn't know what to make of the news of his being taken north. Later, I learned how grateful I should have felt. In North Vietnam he would be in a prison cell which, at least, might provide him with safety from the elements. POWs held by North Vietnamese in the South Vietnam jungles lived in cages and were exposed to the weather—the heat of the sun, humidity, rain, and cold winds. They also faced the probability that those jungle camps would be attacked by our forces not knowing fellow Americans were being held there.

In 1968, when the peace talks began, many of us had hoped the Vietnam War would soon be over. In the fall of 1972, four long years later, the war was still raging. Several times President Nixon halted the bombing of North Vietnam, hoping to bring an end to the war. Each halt stayed in effect for several weeks, but when no progress was made at the negotiating table in Paris, the bombings resumed.

I was in full agreement with President Nixon's method

of trying to secure peace. Henry Kissinger, the American negotiator at the Paris peace talks, was making every effort in his power to reach an agreeable settlement. The last four months of 1972 was one of the most frustrating times for me and for all the families of POWs and MIAs. But I knew they were also frustrating for President Nixon and Mr. Kissinger. One day peace seemed at hand; the next day it was out of reach. Hope one day; the next day all hope dashed.

As we passed the fifth Christmas since Ben's capture, my roller-coaster emotions were frustrating me. Trying to live with one's emotions going up and down is physically draining. I remember saying in a prayer one day in December, "Lord, I don't know how much longer I can hold on."

The National League Committee members had worked long and hard to educate the public about the plight of the POWs and MIAs and had been successful. This was rewarding to us. Our POW/MIA efforts were continuing in full force. We were selling more bracelets than ever, and I continued to make certain I responded to each letter we received from a person who was wearing Ben's bracelet. (If wearers wanted to write to the family of the man whose name was on their bracelet, they sent a letter to the POW/MIA branch of his service. The letter was then forwarded to the family.) I ended each letter with the promise that I would write at least once more, when the POW/MIA issue was resolved. I only hoped my physical and mental strength would hold out for me to see this war come to an end.

When news of a pending peace agreement finally reached the airwaves, I was a target of many reporters who wanted my reaction. No longer did I have to pursue the news media; they pursued me. I received a phone call from a UPI reporter who asked me for my reaction to the announcement of peace. My response was, "I have had my hopes of peace dashed so many times, I refuse to get my hopes up again until I know that peace has been signed."

In January 1973 President Nixon announced to the nation that on January 27 a peace agreement would be signed in

Paris and a list of POWs would be turned over to our government. I was exhilarated! But I had also learned to be cautious.

I hoped I would have good news, but I knew I was facing three possibilities: Ben's name might be on the list; his name might not be on the list; or his name might be on the list of those who had died in POW camp. All I could do was wait a little longer—just a little longer.

23

WAR'S END

In the fall of 1972 new indications that the war was winding down continued to appear on a regular basis. Crisco and his assistant were seen around the camp more frequently. The meals started getting better, and I was even given a small supply of vitamin B-1 to help reduce the swelling in my legs and feet. I was also given permission to start a garden in my cage and was given five garlic bulbs to plant as a start. I separated one of the bulbs into its seven components and planted them. Gene and I shared the remaining four bulbs to add flavor and vitamins to our bland diet.

The attitude of the guards became more tolerant, and Crisco's new assistant, whom I called Harold, actually visited me in my cell. We did a lot of comparing of our two countries, our forms of government, our cultures, and our frustrations. I came to believe that he would have liked to visit America.

The most significant indication that conditions were improving, though, came on the first of November. I was escorted to the camp headquarters building to meet with the camp director. As I walked through the doorway, I saw five other American prisoners. The director, through Crisco, told us that from now on we would be permitted to share a couple of hours and one meal together each week. I wanted to shout with joy but constrained my reaction to a slight smile.

The other Americans were Philip Manhard, U.S. State Department; Eugene Weaver, CIA; Charles Willis, U.S. Voice of America; Captain Theodore Gostas, U.S. Army; and Staff Sergeant Donald Rander, U.S. Army. All five of them had been captured in the city of Hue during the Tet offensive in February 1968.

When we were left alone for a couple of hours, we talked incessantly and learned as much as possible about each other. I learned that prior to their capture all five had been connected in some way to the gathering and evaluating of military intelligence. Crisco's charge that I was an intelligence officer became even more ominous. He must have believed his assertion; why else would I have been put with these five prisoners?

Chuck Willis and Don Rander were occupying a joint cell, thus explaining the conversations in English I had been hearing at K-49.

Phil Manhard startled the rest of us by stating that his cell was adjacent to one occupied by a female prisoner, a nurse from West Germany! Next to her was a male nurse, also from West Germany. Phil had been in contact with the female nurse by written notes exchanged through a small drain hole similar to the one Gene and I had used. The Germans' names were Monika Schwinn and Bernhard Diehl. They were two of the five West German nurses who were captured in South Vietnam while working in a children's hospital under the sponsorship of the Maltese Aid Society, the West German equivalent of the American Red Cross. Three of the five nurses died in the jungles of South Vietnam shortly after capture, but Monika and Bernhard survived and were taken to North Vietnam for detention. Bernhard spoke and wrote English fluently, and this capability made communications between the West Germans and the Americans possible.

There was one other prisoner detained at K-49, but none

of us had any idea who he or she might be. As far as we knew, that person made no effort to get in touch with us.

Phil surprised us a second time asserting, "We have an imposter in our midst." He looked at me and said, "Your name is not Purcell . . . it's Houdini." He went on to explain that it was into his cell at K-77 that I had tossed my note during my escape in December 1969. He told us the camp authorities reacted to my escape by having a trustee nail extra boards over the panels in the doors of all the cells.

Phil also told me about another prisoner who was transferred to K-77 from the Hanoi Hilton in January 1970 as punishment. His name was Kenneth R. Hughey, Major, USAF. There was a common wall separating their two courtyards but it wasn't long before they were communicating via the tap code which was a part of a pilot's survival training.

They first exchanged personal data such as name, service number and physical condition then went on to identify other POWs that each of them knew. Phil then told Ken about my escape from cell 18 in early December. Major Hughey returned to the Hanoi Hilton a few weeks later and entered all our names into the network, a list of names of all U.S. prisoners within the greater Hanoi prison system.

Apparently the Vietnamese prison guards also became aware of the above information because upon my return to America in the spring of 1973 I was told by a defense intelligence official that I probably would have been executed as an escapee had the Vietnamese not known that my name had been circulated. Thank goodness for my afterthought.

After we were served the standard lunch, we all returned to our respective cells with a much higher expectation that peace and freedom would follow soon. The ensuing week seemed to drag more than usual as I waited for the next opportunity to meet with my five new friends. (The West Germans met with each other at the same time, but we could not visit with them.)

In preparing for the next meeting I wrote a note that I asked Phil to pass through Monika to Bernhard. I had no idea at that time why the Germans were with us, but the Vietnamese officials must have suspected that they were somehow connected with the U.S. intelligence effort in South Vietnam. In any event, in my capacity as the senior military officer present, I extended to Bernhard an offer to speak to the camp authorities on their behalf, should they need medicine, food, water, or other help. Phil agreed to pass the note.

When we met a week later, Phil handed me a note from Bernhard in which he expressed his appreciation for my offer but politely refused to accept it. He considered it improper to be associated with an American serviceman in any capacity.

What surprised me most about this event was that Phil asserted that he, as a senior State Department official, was in charge of the American prisoners at K-49, not I. This assertion blew my mind, to use the vernacular of the time. Phil and I continued to discuss the issue heatedly for two more weeks until I proposed a compromise, which he was willing to accept.

"Since we are prisoners in a Communist country, and since military forces in a Communist country have both a unit commander and a political commissar, I'll be the unit commander of this outfit and you will serve as the political commissar."

We were both absolutely certain that when we returned to America, the departments of State and Defense would study this issue and reach a decision as to who is responsible for American lives in a prisoner-of-war camp, the senior civilian or the senior combat arms officer. At our level of responsibility we could argue the question for years without ever resolving it, but the larger question is, Who does the President hold responsible for the welfare of American citizens? Within a combat zone the answer to this question seems crystal clear to me. The senior military prisoner must assume that responsibility until relieved by higher authority.

On the twenty-third of December I was moved from my old cell to the cell previously occupied by Phil. Therefore, I became the channel of communication between the Americans and the two West Germans.

On the twenty-sixth of December I began my third hunger strike to protest my continued solitary confinement and my inability to write a letter to my wife. For thirteen days I refused to accept the meals that were offered. In the two previous strikes my drinking water was cut off within a day after I refused the first meal, but that reaction would not have been effective on this occasion since I had a large reservoir of water in the toilet. To be sure, this reservoir of water had not been purified by boiling, but I could drink it in an emergency.

Another reason that I was able to go thirteen days this time without taking food from my captors was that whenever I met with the other Americans they would bring some of their bread and some rice provided by Monika.

Crisco and Harold tried to reason with me and said I would become ill if I didn't eat. I do believe they were concerned for my physical condition, but I was never certain for what reason. One guard even tried to encourage me to eat by bringing me a piece of sugar cane. To turn down that treat took every ounce of resistance I could muster.

Two events finally convinced me to end my hunger strike. The first was Crisco's promise to check with the authorities in Hanoi and ask for permission for me to write to my family. This was the first time that he actually promised to at least seek permission. Secondly, on the sixth of January a guard brought into my cell a pan of fried potatoes, and the desire to eat something fried was simply overwhelming. I had never been served any fried food until that time.

Although I enjoyed the fried potatoes, I was disappointed that I was still not permitted to write to Anne. I had hopes, though, that permission would come through shortly—perhaps in time for my twenty-first wedding anniversary.

I realized that on the twentieth of January, 1973, Anne and I would have been married for twenty-one years, and I had been away from home because of military service for seven of those years, or exactly one third of the total time.

Late in the afternoon of the twenty-sixth of January one of the guards came into my cell and handed me a sheet of paper and a pencil. He then announced, "You may write to your wife."

I choked up at those words and realized that I couldn't utter anything except a very soft "thank you."

I had waited 1,814 days for just such an opportunity, and now here it was at last. The surprise, the sheer joy that I experienced at that moment, made me feel weak in the knees and a bit lightheaded. I sat down on the stool to recover my composure, laid the paper and pencil on the small table, and started trying to collect my thoughts for an actual letter . . . but words simply would not come to my mind.

What should I write after so many years of total separation? Which of the many experiences were worth using a few precious lines of paper to share with my family? Would I have another opportunity to write soon, or was this the only chance I'd have until the war ended? Finally I decided to give up even trying to sort out the questions now but to sleep on them. I went to bed, but sleep didn't come all that easily.

As soon as it was light enough to see on the morning of the twenty-seventh, I was up and seated at the table. I started writing. Words printed with very small letters began to fill the page. I wrote briefly about my capture and then moved on to subjects of health, hope, and love. To assure Anne that I was the one writing the letter I included many personal comments and facts which only I could possibly know. I told her that my health was reasonably good and then began to ask questions that screamed for answers: How is your health? Where are you and the children living now? How are they doing? What can you tell me about Mom? Have you heard any news about my situation before this letter? When will this war end?

When the page was completely filled with words, I turned it over and wrote all I could on the reverse side. Then I read it and reread it several times. I signed it the way we had told each other good night every night of our married life: "I love you, Anne, and I'm not mad at you. Good night." This was because we had vowed long ago never to go to sleep angry with each other.

The warm tropical sun was directly overhead when the guard delivered my noon meal. He placed the food on the table and picked up the letter. For some reason he was in a very happy mood, and so was I. Was he happy because he had been promoted? Or was he going home on a pass? The answer to my question wasn't long in coming.

After I finished my meal and took the usual noontime nap, the guard returned to my cell and directed that I follow him to the camp headquarters building.

What now, I wondered. Was something wrong with the letter? Had the authorities changed their minds? Had I written something that caused Crisco to get upset? These thoughts and many more crossed my mind on the way to the camp headquarters building that afternoon.

As I entered the building I saw the other five American prisoners; Crisco; the camp director; and another Vietnamese, who, judging from the attitude of the camp director, held some position of importance.

Crisco interpreted as the official spoke.

"I have good news," he said. "Your government and the governments of the Democratic Republic of Vietnam and the Provisional Revolutionary Government of South Vietnam have agreed to conditions to end the war and restore peace to Vietnam. These agreements call for the exchange of all persons detained by either side."

The camp director then said, "Congratulations. As soon as you finish your evening meal you will be taken to Hanoi to prepare for your release."

The six of us sat quietly in stunned disbelief. I stared at the other five prisoners, and the gleam in their hollow eyes spoke volumes. We had been subjected to five years of isolation, maltreatment, threats, and terrible living conditions. But today was the beginning of the end. At long last we could see a ray of light at the end of the tunnel.

We all stood and shook hands with each other and then with our captors. As we returned to our individual cells to await the evening meal and the trip to Hanoi, we were euphoric.

After dark we six Americans, along with Crisco, a driver, and two guards, loaded into a small military vehicle and departed K-49 for the final time. Along the way we did a lot of talking and laughing, and those in the group who smoked were given all the cigarettes they wanted.

We traveled almost two hours in a southerly direction before we entered the metropolitan area of Hanoi and, shortly thereafter, the Hao Loa prison, better known as the "Hanoi Hilton."

That night, after spending fifty-eight months without a cellmate, I was placed in a community cell with other Americans. I would spend the final days as a prisoner of war with friends.

I was no longer alone!

24

NEWS

Saturday, January 27, was a long, long day. The peace agreements were to be signed in Paris that morning, and I hoped to have the information about Ben by mid-afternoon. It was the day I had lived and worked for, and I was so full of nervous energy that even while the day was still young I managed to accomplish many of the household chores I had been ignoring.

My mother and my Aunt Ethel drove down to be with us during this time, and I was grateful for their presence. At least they were calm enough to look after the needs of my children.

Colonel Don Gluck, my FSAO, would be the first one to receive the information about Ben. He was remaining close to his home phone. I learned later that others were being inconvenienced by the delay in receiving our message: Colonel Gluck's teenage daughter wasn't allowed to use the phone all day.

Mid-afternoon came and went with no message. At 6:00 P.M. a car with four Gold Star Wives drove into my driveway. Before I had known the peace accords would be signed on January 27, I had made plans to go out for dinner and a play with my friends. They understood when I told them I was much too nervous to eat dinner. However, I planned to join them later at the theater if I had not received word about Ben by then. I felt a need to get out of the house. This had been a "year-long" day.

I called Colonel Gluck shortly after 6:30 P.M. He still had heard nothing. I told him that I planned to attend the play and where I would be sitting. We agreed that if I didn't hear from him before the play ended, I would call him when I got back home.

The play was beginning when I arrived at the theater. Our seats were in the balcony and difficult to get to, but I found my friends and sat in the aisle seat they had saved for me. I suppose it was a good play—the audience seemed to be enjoying it—but I had no idea at all what was going on on-stage. I was just as miserable here as I would have been at home. The play seemed to drag on and on, and I was becoming more nervous by the minute.

Then I saw Colonel Gluck, who with the assistance of an usher was making his way slowly toward my seat. I couldn't move. As I watched him, I thought perhaps I could tell by the expression on his face what he had to tell me. He would be a good poker player because I saw absolutely nothing there.

Breathing a quick prayer, I decided I wouldn't say or ask anything until he told me all that he knew. I felt like an actress in a play of my own, but very few people around us were aware of our performance. He came to my seat, took me by the arm, and led me back along the same slow route out of the balcony until we reached the stairwell.

There, he gave my arm a little squeeze and said, "It's good news, Anne. But Ben's name is on the civilian list, and because we don't understand why you must not tell anyone about this."

I could not believe my ears! I wouldn't have to tell anyone; they could simply look at my smiling face and know that Ben was coming home!

Suddenly I was aware that my friend Zema Laird had followed us to the stairwell and was standing a short distance away. I appreciated her caring enough to be near if I needed

her. If it had been bad news she would have definitely understood, for she had already traveled that road. I turned and
went to her and gave her a bear hug. I didn't say anything;
she knew.

Colonel Gluck walked with me to my car and asked if I
could make it home.

"Sure," I said. After all, I had lived in Columbus for four
years and seven months now. Suddenly I gasped, unaccount-
ably remembering the dream I had had at Mom's during the
summer of 1968! Now I knew what the 47 meant. It meant
four years and seven months since the night of my dream.

Despite my assurances that I could get home okay, in
my rush to be there when Colonel Gluck told our family
the news, I took a wrong turn. As a result, I rambled
around for a short while in an unfamiliar part of town,
and by the time I arrived home the family had already
been told. I noticed, though, that they were all crying. For
a split second I was frightened that, somehow, I must have
misunderstood the message. Then I realized that the tears
were tears of joy.

Our TV was on, and as each Georgia POW's family
was notified the POW's name was run in a crawl across
the bottom of the screen. Several names were already running, and silently I rejoiced with each of those families, all
friends now, as they received the news. The National
League of Families had made us into a close-knit group.
We had shared the suffering; now we were able to share
the happiness.

I learned in the midst of the joy of my own upcoming
reunion that Doris's husband John would not be coming
home. He was still MIA. My heart went out to Doris and
thousands of others like her whose husbands' names were not
on the list of returning prisoners of war, and I felt guilty for
being the one who received the good news.

I knew the news media would be calling soon for our
reaction, and that was to be expected. Once, when contem-
plating what it might be like when Ben returned, I had found
a nice quiet spot in a nearby town where the children and I
could go to get away from everything for a while. I thought
of that place now, as I knew the media would be making demands that could be taxing on all of us.

I asked Colonel Gluck how we were going to handle the gag order we had received from the Department of the Army. He spent a long time on our phone and after a while came back with a solution. I could tell family and friends, but I couldn't go public with any remarks to the media until further notification.

Our local media had been great to us when we needed information published or coverage for our projects. But the media in Atlanta had ignored many of our projects and requests to help educate the public about the plight of our men. Other things had been more important to them. The ball was in my court now, and I thought it might be fun to play hard to get.

The game lasted only three days; then the Department of the Army cleared me to speak publicly. They had finally decided that it would not jeopardize any future releases—the last thing any of us would have wanted to happen.

The slowness in getting notification to me on the twenty-seventh was due not only to Ben's name being on the civilian list but also to the fact that there was a *Bob* Purcell on the list. Colonel Bob Purcell, U.S. Air Force, had a birthday on February 14. Colonel Ben Purcell, U.S. Army, had a birthday on February 14. Bob Purcell had a wife named Mary Ann; Ben's wife was named Eleanor Anne; Bob had five children. Ben had five children. These unusual coincidences presented some questions at the Department of the Army and the Department of the Air Force. They didn't want to give either of our families erroneous information.

That very night we began to receive phone calls from people who were rejoicing with us, and in the days that followed letters and cards expressing happiness poured in. People who had worn POW bracelets with Ben's name on them returned them to us with words of gratitude for the sacrifice he had made for our country. I began to put my thoughts together so that I could write one more time, as I had promised, to each person who had worn Ben's bracelet.

I had had an extremely large support team: friends, who made me laugh; Ola, who made me work; family, who made me feel loved; and the church, which was there when I needed it. Until Ben's return I didn't know that he also had had a support team—the chicken who helped him escape, the ants who caused an argument between him and Gene Weaver, a dead mouse hung in the peephole of his cell, and the low-flying pilot of that timely Phantom Jet.

The most-asked question of the reporters was, "When do you think Colonel Purcell will be home?"

My answer was, "All prisoners are to be released within sixty days. What are sixty days compared to five years?"

I found those next sixty days to be an eternity.

Groups of POWs were being released about every ten to fourteen days. The waiting to see if Ben's name would be on the next release list was emotional enough, but when releases were delayed on several occasions and the North Vietnamese threatened to curtail releases altogether, my emotions would take a real nosedive. Those were sixty days of roller-coaster nerves! I had a card—I think it came from *Guideposts* magazine—that said, "God is in control. Expect a miracle." I kept that card on my dresser and looked at it often. It helped keep me on track.

The second-most-asked question was, "What do you think the colonel will want when he gets home?"

I could think of several things, a few of which I chose not to reveal publicly. But knowing how much Ben liked watermelon I said "Watermelon. I'm sure he hasn't had any watermelon in five years."

It wasn't watermelon season, so as I answered the question I figured Ben would have to wait a little longer. But my comment was read by the president of the Watermelon Growers' Association of America, who lived in South Carolina. He called me and said he was having three melons flown from Mexico City to Columbus, Georgia, just for Ben. I knew Ben would be delighted to have a watermelon cutting in early spring instead of having to wait until summertime.

The watermelons arrived in February, and the manager of a Piggly Wiggly food market told me I could keep them in the store's cooler indefinitely. I still didn't know when Ben would be released.

During those sixty days many things were going on in our

lives. Sherri broke her arm at school—the first broken bone any of our children had ever had. David's girlfriend, Sandy Ortiz, decorated the cast and printed a big "Welcome Home Daddy" on it. A news photographer took a picture of Sherri with her "cast sign," and her picture went out all over the United States. When Ben came home, Sherri wore her sign to meet her dad.

I was busy getting a dress made and buying new things for the children to wear to our reunion. I replaced the long-sleeved night gown I had been wearing with a very pretty, pink-lace short one. And I purchased some lovely new sheets for our bed. The living room sofa was re-covered, and our antique French floor lamp got a new shade. How things looked had begun to matter again.

Everywhere we went, people would rejoice with us. The war had dragged on for such a long time that people were ready to hear something good coming out of Vietnam.

The Department of the Army sent me a letter giving permission to send a package to Ben at Clark Air Force Base in the Philippines. I decided to send some pictures and a letter, which I called my brag sheets, to bring him up-to-date on each of us. I thought this might make homecoming a little easier for him.

Once prisoners started to be released, I began receiving calls from a few of them. Quincy Collins, a Georgia returnee, called to tell me Ben was well and had "gone over the wall twice." At first I didn't know what he meant. Then I realized he meant that Ben had escaped twice. I always felt that if at all possible Ben would keep himself busy. But I never dreamed he would busy himself in that way. My first reaction was to be thankful Ben had not been shot for escaping.

Joe Rose, the warrant officer who had been flying the helicopter that had crashed, called to tell me that Ben was feeling fine. Joe also told me he and his fiancée were getting married *right away*. In a time when many young women felt they couldn't wait one year for their men to return from a normal Vietnam tour, Donna had waited *five* years—but they weren't waiting any longer.

One evening Colonel Gluck called and asked me to meet

secretly with him and a colonel from the Department of the Army. I made the necessary arrangements, and when I arrived at Colonel Gluck's office at Fort Benning the Army Department colonel gave me a letter from Ben. It was on a small piece of paper in very tiny handwriting to save space. Ben told me that he had not been well and that he was anxious to get home. He asked me to call the wife of a POW named Ted Gostas. He said to tell her that Ted was sick and to be prepared for this when Ted was released. Ben wrote that Ted should have been on the first release, and that he was trying to get him on the next list coming out.

The Army colonel asked me not to notify Ted's wife but to let the Department of the Army do it. He also asked me to keep the letter a secret from everyone. Then he said he had a letter for Ben's mom, and he wanted my opinion as to her ability to keep it secret. I told him I didn't think Mom could do that. He gave me the letter and asked me to use my best judgment about giving it to her. I decided I would not, since she knew by now that Ben was coming home. I knew Ben would understand when I explained my reason.

I never dreamed how difficult it would be for me to finally have a letter after all these years but not be able to tell anyone. The next day I called Colonel Gluck and explained to him how much difficulty I was having not being able to share the news. I asked him to come out and read my letter. Since he already knew about the letter, that wouldn't be breaking any promises.

Once the letter had been shared with him, I no longer felt the need to tell anyone else.

The reason I was asked not to tell anyone about the letters was because they had been slipped out by a German nurse when she was released. Once she reached Clark base, she had given them to our authorities, who had them flown to Washington immediately. There, the letters were read and then brought to me. The Department of the Army was afraid that if the North Vietnamese learned information was being slipped out, they might hold up future releases, or worse, stop them entirely.

One of the newspaper pictures that tugged most at my Heart was that of Dick Ziegler meeting his five-year-old son for the first time. His son was born after Dick left for Vietnam. Dick had been the copilot of Ben's helicopter, and his wife had committed suicide about a year and a half after Dick was captured. When I heard about her death shortly after it happened, I wished I could have been near her to give her support, hope, and a will to live.

There was a special ceremony honoring POWs and MIAs, sponsored by the city of Columbus in February, and as that event was breaking up Mayor J. R. Allen told me he was very anxious to meet Ben. He had faithfully worn Ben's bracelet for many months and had supported our POW efforts locally as well as statewide. Tragically, a few days later Mayor Allen was killed in a plane crash near Rome, Georgia. It was a terrible loss for his family and our city. I was sorry Ben would not have the privilege of meeting him.

I eagerly awaited each new list. Families were notified about a week prior to their loved one's release. The arrival of the first returnees was broadcast live from Clark Air Force Base as the men descended the steps of their U.S. Air Force transport planes. It was shown on American TV in the wee hours of the morning. I stayed awake to see each man arrive and cried tears of joy for each family.

Many of the returnees I knew by name only, from seeing their names on the POW/MIA bracelets. But I felt I knew them personally since all our families had for so long a time shared this experience.

Finally it was our turn! David was home on spring break from the U.S. Military Academy, so the entire family was together. We were notified that Ben would be leaving Hanoi on March 27. I requested that Colonel Gluck call me as soon as he knew Ben had actually left North Vietnam. Usually, if the FSAO received notification after 9:00 P.M. the family wasn't notified until 7:00 A.M. the next morning. I asked him not to wait overnight. It was very important for me to know when Ben was no longer in North Vietnamese territory.

The phone call finally came at just a little past 2:30 A.M. on March 27. Colonel Gluck's voice said, "Anne, Ben has cleared North Vietnamese air space and is on a plane to Clark Air Base."

At that moment, and not until that moment, I knew for sure Ben was on his way home! I went running through the house screaming over and over again, "Ben is no longer a prisoner of war! Ben is no longer a prisoner of war!"

I shook the children until they were all awake and we cried and hugged and danced all over the house.

Ben was coming home, and he was on his way! Our war was finally coming to an end.

True to the scripture in James 1:2–5, God had given me strength to face my problems, helped me grow in patience, and led me through these years with his wisdom.

25

THE HANOI HILTON

BEN'S STORY

For the first week after we arrived at the Hanoi Hilton, our food was much as it had been, although the amount was increased. Shortly after we arrived we were even served a fatty portion of meat, but whether it was pork or beef I didn't know. The truth was it had been so long since I had tasted meat of any kind that I could no longer tell the difference.

When the six of us who left K-49 arrived at the Hanoi Hilton, we were split up within the cell block and assigned to one of three rooms containing six or eight wooden cots each. I was placed in a room with Staff Sergeant Don Rander, Captain Ted Gostas, and Captain Jim Thompson, the same person I had met on the trail from Bao Cao to K-77 in July 1968—the man who by now had spent more time as a prisoner of war than any serviceman in our nation's history. It was certainly good to see Jim again.

Also in the room with me were two U.S. civilians, Lewis Meyers and Clodeon "Speed" Adkins. Both of these civilian "detainees" had displayed the true American spirit by escaping with Jim Thompson two years earlier. But that's a story they will have to tell.

Twenty other prisoners from various outlying camps were also brought into our cell block at this time. At the end of a hallway within the cell block was a fourth large room. It was to this room, divided by a partition, that Bernhard Diehl and Monika Schwinn were assigned. Within three days we made face-to-face contact with Bernhard and Monika and discovered that there was a third prisoner in the room, a Canadian citizen named Marc Cayer. Marc had been working in South Vietnam as an agricultural specialist when he was taken prisoner during the Tet offensive of 1968.

Perhaps we should be surprised to learn that the Vietnamese government ignored accepted international norms governing the treatment of prisoners of war by holding noncombatants in the same prison system with combat troops. However, as the world now knows, Communist governments operate on a different set of rules—rules they will pledge to other nations to keep but then set aside if they perceive an advantage in doing so. In our case I believe we were all *hostages* in the real sense of that term.

The camp authorities rushed us through a very cursory physical and dental exam. My physical condition seemed to be fair, but my teeth needed a lot of work after five years of no checkups and a poor diet. The dental technician used a small, spoon-shaped instrument to dig out the decay from two of my teeth, without benefit of any anesthetic, and then packed a white substance into the cavities. It didn't feel very good, but at least I could chew my food now.

There was a great deal of laughing and talking within our common room. We also went to other rooms to swap tales. My own story of the sudden appearance of the F-4 Phantom jet during one of Crisco's interrogations brought a few laughs, as did the tale of my "watch-chicken." Most, however, seemed to like the story of Charlie, the dummy, best.

"Ben, couldn't you have just arranged for Charlie to take a leak on one of the guards?" one of the men asked.

During the first week after our arrival we were informed by the camp director, through Crisco, that we would all be released within sixty days of January 27. There would be four releases at two-week intervals. Any sick or wounded would be in the first release, and others would follow in sequence of dates of capture.

Crisco asked if anyone would like to take a tour of down-town Hanoi, and sixteen of us indicated that we would like to do so. Early the next morning two guards delivered eight blue suits, eight shirts, and eight pairs of shoes to our building. The first eight men to go on the tour picked over the clothes until they found a reasonable fit. As soon as they were dressed, they boarded a mid-sized military vehicle and departed the Hilton. Within three hours they returned, removed their fancy duds, and passed them on to the second group. I was a member of the second group.

For me it was a strange feeling to put on a pair of shoes, a shirt, and trousers. I was very self-conscious about the way I looked and I almost backed out. One man did back out, so our group had only seven men instead of the intended eight.

As we departed the Hilton and drove a few miles through the city of Hanoi, the canvas side and rear curtains on the vehicle were lowered. I could see very little of the city as I bent over to look toward the front, through the cab and wind-shield, but it was apparent that most of the people were either walking or riding bicycles. There were very few motor vehi-cles on the streets.

Our first stop was near a large body of water. Crisco told us it was a very old and famous lake with a floating pagoda in the middle of it. I had never heard of it before, and I wasn't too impressed. The people we met as we walked to and from the lake were very polite but cool. I felt certain they didn't realize we were American prisoners of war.

Our second and only other stop was at a public park where the remains of an American B-52 were on display. Though there was very little else to look at I enjoyed just being outside the confines of a prison wall. As our group strolled through the park with escorts (guards without weap-ons), we met one very young man wearing a military uniform. He must have thought we were important dignitaries, perhaps from the Soviet Union, because he saluted us as we ap-proached. Although it had been years since I had been sa-luted, my military experience and training dictated a snappy salute in return. As we walked farther along the trail, I noticed one of our escorts chewing out that young soldier. But to have been saluted, even erroneously, was a good feeling for an old soldier.

Early on the eighth of February, right after breakfast, Crisco called me out to a small interrogation room. He handed me the letter that I had written to Anne back at K-49 and said, "This letter is much too long. You may write only six lines and you can speak only about your health and personal greetings."

Crisco provided me with a smaller sheet of paper and a regular ink pen and instructed me to rewrite the letter. The first letter had been difficult to write, but that was no challenge compared with trying to put my thoughts down in the space of only six lines. In the knowledge that we would all be released soon, I did my best with the six lines and returned the letter to Crisco.

For two weeks we had received double rations, along with rudimentary medical and dental care, and apparently were found fit enough to join a larger group of prisoners. On the ninth of February our entire group, including the foreign nationals, was moved into another cell block of the Hilton.

As I passed through the door leading into the larger compound, a short, very thin young man approached me. I could tell by the look in his eyes that he had something he wanted to share with me, but at first I didn't recognize him. Then I realized that it was Warrant Officer Joe Rose, the pilot who had been flying the helicopter when we were shot down five years and one day earlier.

"Colonel, I'm sorry," Joe said. "I was flying at the wrong altitude. It's bothered me for five years that I contributed to our being here."

"Joe, what's done is done. We're going home," I replied. "Let's just thank the Lord that we have survived the ordeal."

Then Joe asked, "Have you heard from your wife?"

"No," I said. "Not one word in five years and one day."

"Well, I heard over the camp radio in December that a UPI reporter had interviewed the wife of a Colonel Ben Purcell," Joe said. "She had been asked what she thought about the rumors that the war was about over, and she had responded by saying, 'I've had my hopes up so many times, only to have them dashed, that I refuse to get them up again until I know peace is really here.' "

That report from Mr. Rose told me two things that I hadn't known for sure until that day. First, Anne was alive. Second, I could presume she was in good health or else she wouldn't have been interviewed. Five years and one day without a single word from Anne or any indication that she was alive and well! I wondered if she too had had to live those years without knowing whether she was a wife or a widow.

In the larger compound I met all the men who had been with me on the trail from South Vietnam, plus many others. There were 106 prisoners in this particular cell block. Eighty had been there before our arrival, to which had been added our group of twenty-six. Crisco said that all in our group were prisoners of the PRG, the Provisional Revolutionary Government of South Vietnam.

Bernhard Diehl was assigned to a cell with seven of us, whereas Monika Schwinn was in a nearby cell by herself. Monika was allowed to visit Bernhard in our cell during mealtimes, and this was good for the rest of us cruddy old men. As Monika approached our cell, we would put on our jackets and stand to welcome her, and of course she would be the first to take her meal from the table. It was good to have a refresher course in gentlemanly behavior.

Not only was Monika the one spot of beauty in an otherwise drab crowd, she had also demonstrated a high degree of courage and willingness to take personal risks for the benefit of other prisoners. In addition to passing notes between prisoners at K-49, Monika had shared her meager ration of rice with me while I was on my third hunger strike. Here in the Hilton she continued to help others in any way possible.

When Monika learned that she would be released four weeks before me, she offered to take out of the prison any notes I wanted to send. I gave her three: one to Anne, one to my mother, and one to the American authorities at Clark Air Force Base informing them of Captain Gostas's urgent need for medical and dental treatment. (Captain Gostas was scheduled to be released in the last group, on March 27.)

Monika told me later she had opened a seam in the collar

of her blouse and inserted the notes in the collar. But three days later a guard brought her a new blouse for the trip home and asked for the old one. Monika told the guard she would need time to change and that he would have to come back later for the old blouse. Quickly she removed the notes, hid them under the cardboard liner of her small handbag, restitched the collar, and then summoned the guard to come get her old blouse. During all this she was as "cool as a cucumber."

Around February 18 we heard quite a commotion coming from the section of the Hilton where all the pilots were being detained. Apparently a group of these pilots were leaving for home and wanted to tell the entire world. We who remained did not blame them one bit for rejoicing. Later the grapevine confirmed that although more than one hundred pilots were freed, not one prisoner from our cell block had been released.

Why was this? Had something gone wrong? Was the South Vietnamese Revolutionary Government being obstinate about our release? Those of us who were technically prisoners of the PRG felt a degree of anxiety over what we thought was a stupid arrangement. Although we were all being detained in Hanoi, the PRG was using us to force Washington to deal with them as a political entity. Had Washington refused? Were we to be the pawns in this terrible game?

Our fears proved unfounded. We learned that a number of prisoners of the PRG who had been held in the jungle border areas between South Vietnam and Cambodia were released the next day. The plan called for three more releases about two weeks apart. Each release would contain approximately one-third of the pilots and one-third of our group. We couldn't argue with this system, but we would have preferred that all of us depart at the same time.

When I was first transferred into this larger compound on February 9, I met an Air Force officer named Ted Guy. He had been serving as SRO (Senior Responsible Officer) to the group of eighty or so prisoners who had been together for several months preceding the signing of the Paris Peace Accords. We compared data and backgrounds and discovered that I had been senior in rank to him on the date of our re-

spective shootdowns—mine in February, his in April of 1968.
Since normal operating procedures dictated that the most senior officer on that date of the shootdown be responsible for
the welfare of other Americans in a situation such as we were
in, I assumed overall responsibility for the 106 prisoners while
Ted retained direct responsibility for the original eighty. Phillip Manhard continued in his role as spokesman for the U.S.
civilians.

When the rosters of the future releases were made public
I noticed that I was scheduled to be released on March 13
and Ted Guy on March 27. I told Crisco that I was going to
remain at the Hilton until the last American was freed—that
Ted could go on the thirteenth in my place. Crisco was very
upset and a bit worried about the prospect of having to tell
the camp director of this latest problem created by Purcell.
He said, "You must go when we say."

"You can tie me up and carry me to the point of release
if you so decide, but I'm not leaving on my own," I replied.

Two days later the names were switched on the roster.

I had a very strong conviction that I should not accept
release until I was certain, to the extent possible under very
adverse conditions, that all other Americans were already released or that they were going out with me. My exchange with
Guy meant a two-week delay in my departure, but for me the
issue was one of professional responsibility, of leadership, and
of personal honor. Those qualities had always been very important to me and were now more important than ever.

Shortly after I was placed in the larger compound I received a report from Colonel Guy that there were eight
Americans among us who were referred to as privileged characters (PCs for short). As a group they had over the years
been allowed to work in the kitchen and the aid station, receiving special attention in both of those areas. Some of the
PCs had made propaganda tapes and at least one was reported to have given instruction on how to identify American
aircraft to the prison officials and/or guards. King David Rayford was one of those PCs.

One day when I was locked in my cell while he and the
other PCs had access to the courtyard, he stopped by to talk
with me. He told me that he was reluctant to accept release

and return to America for fear of "getting into hot water" over his conduct while in prison. He also told me the Vietnamese authorities had said that they had to turn him over to the American authorities but that if he desired to remain in Vietnam, he could "make a dash for it" *after* he had been officially turned over and he would be granted asylum. I advised King that he would be better off taking his chance with the American judicial system if need be than to remain in Vietnam. He must have heeded my advice, for he was returned to U.S. control and subsequently released from the army without any judicial action being taken against him.

Crisco and the other interpreters continued their practice of calling their assigned prisoners out for discussions. On one occasion Don Rander and I were in just such a meeting when Crisco gave each of us a bottle of beer. Before we could open the bottle, a photographer entered the room and prepared his camera to take some pictures. As we reached for the bottle, the photographer would aim his camera at us. Don and I would take our hands from the table, and the photographer would drop his camera. It was readily apparent that the authorities wanted to get some shots of American POWs drinking beer. This type of photograph would give the Vietnamese a good propaganda shot to show the world how gemütlich their treatment of Americans had really been.

Don and I both recognized their ploy and decided to make a game out of the process. Repeatedly we'd reach for the beer, then withdraw our hands before the photographer could shoot the picture. After almost an hour of this cat-and-mouse exercise Crisco told us to return to our cells. The bottles of beer stayed on the table unopened.

One day Bernhard and Monika had been out for one of these discussion sessions, during which the Vietnamese were trying to convince them that their treatment had not been bad all these years. Bernhard would have nothing to do with their hypocritical effort. The only mistake these two fine people had made was to try and help the sick children of South Vietnam, and for that they had been subjected to years of brutal imprisonment. As he returned to our cell he was visibly upset—fed up with the camp authorities would be a more accurate description. He walked straight over to me, snapped to attention, saluted smartly, and said, "Colonel, I place myself under your command."

In truth, I never understood exactly what Bernhard meant by that, but from that moment on we coordinated our efforts to "bug" the enemy.

Three or four days before Bernhard was to be released he was moved from our cell into a larger holding cell along with the thirty or so prisoners who were scheduled for the next release. The overhead light burned brightly in that cell all night, and the other prisoners, excited about their impending departure, jabbered incessantly. Bernhard could get no rest, so the next morning he simply moved back into my cell without asking permission. The camp director was furious over this display of "bad attitude." We all had a hearty laugh over it.

Later that day I was moved, along with four other Americans, into another cell block on the opposite side of the prison known as New Guy Village. It was in this cell that most of the newly captured pilots were placed while undergoing initial interrogations. There were still many visible signs of the bad treatment and torture which had taken place within these walls. Leg stocks and wall hooks were still in place. I saw that the cells had neither windows nor ventilation holes. Such a place, I knew for a fact, could get very steamy in the hot summer afternoons. The walls were covered with large globs of plaster, which served as soundproofing. This was to deaden the sound of screams from the Americans who were punished in the torture cells for refusing to cooperate with the camp authorities.

With me in New Guy Village were captains Jim Thompson and Ted Gostas, Staff Sergeant Don Rander, and a civilian, Chuck Willis. The only plausible reason for the five of us to have been moved was to separate us from Bernhard, who would return from his discussion to an empty cell.

The second day in New Guy Village brought a bit of excitement. Shortly before lunch we heard someone whistling the tune "The Streets of Laredo." I moved to the rear of our cell, which faced the fourteen-foot-high outer perimeter wall of the prison. From here I would have a better chance of communicating with the whistling person, whom I presumed to be an American.

"Who is that whistling?" I called.

"Commander Phillip A. Kientzler, U.S. Navy."

"Where are you?" I called.

"I'm in cell number one . . . in solitary."

"When were you captured?"

"Twenty-seven January."

"I mean what year?"

"This year," Phillip responded.

"This year?" I replied incredulously.

Phillip had taken off from his aircraft carrier for a mission over Quang Tri Province early on the very morning the Paris Peace Accords were to be signed. He was shot down just south of the demilitarized zone (DMZ). Talk about unfortunate timing . . . how could this have been worse? He was captured almost immediately after hitting the ground and transported by a small jeeplike vehicle across the DMZ. Just north of the DMZ he was loaded aboard a small aircraft and flown directly to Hanoi, where he was placed in cell one of New Guy Village. He was told that since his name was not on the list turned over to the American authorities in Paris earlier that day, he might never go home. Certainly he would not go home until he confessed his crimes against the Vietnamese people and refirmed his thinking.

At that moment Phillip was a very concerned young man, and we had to do something to try and help him.

I asked the other guys to join with me in a protest by refusing to eat our meals, and they all agreed. When we refused our first meal the guard took away our drinking water, but this time it didn't bother us a bit. The monsoon rains were coming down in torrents and running off the roof about three feet in front of our cell door. I ripped a one-inch-by-two-inch wooden strip off the back of our door and used it as a handle to extend our drinking cups out under the downspout. We had all the fresh rainwater we needed. This procedure went on for three days before we were moved back into the larger cell block.

Within an hour after we were resettled, Chuck, Don, and

I were taken in for interrogation. The camp director, with Crisco translating, wanted to know why we weren't eating. I answered for the three of us.

"We are protesting the treatment of another American prisoner named Phillip Kientzler."

"That isn't your business," Crisco said. "Besides, we are providing you with good treatment."

I was tense and irritable from hunger pains, and my condition led me to blow my top in response to such a stupid statement.

"Bullshit," I said. "You know that's a lie."

As Crisco translated my response the camp director's face went red. He jumped to his feet, shouted at me, and then gave instructions to the guard who was standing behind me. The guard chambered a round in his AK-47 and placed the muzzle at the base of my head.

Chuck and Don sat quietly on their stools wondering what was coming next, and I have to confess that I wasn't exactly a disinterested party myself. After a long, anxious moment the camp director said something again and the gun was lowered. Crisco ordered us to return to our cells, and as we walked out of the room I heard Chuck let out a big sigh of relief.

The next day Phillip Kientzler joined our group. He was in a talkative mood, and it was two days before he finished answering all of our questions about the outside world. Those were interesting days for us, darkened only by the fact that my friends Bernhard and Monika had been released while my group was in New Guy Village, robbing me of the opportunity to tell them farewell.

During our four-day absence from the larger compound all the other prisoners had received packages from the American Red Cross. It was three more days before our packages were given to us. My package was addressed to *Colonel* Ben Purcell, U.S. Army. Was this an error, or had I been promoted? I hoped for the latter.

I didn't concern myself with this question for very long but proceeded to dig into my first package since Christmas of 1967. It contained a variety of items long absent from my life. I went for the crackers and cheese spread first because it was on top. A cup of instant coffee really hit the spot. After ten thousand cups of plain hot water the flavor of coffee was absolutely delicious.

As I dug deeper into the box I found a bottle of Coricidin, which I mistook for multiple vitamin pills. Shortly after taking four tablets and becoming very sleepy, I was told by Major Hal Kushner, a U.S. Army flight surgeon when captured, that this was a cold preparation containing aspirin and antihistamine. I discarded the remainder of the Coricidin and kept looking for vitamins, but there were none in the package. I did find a new Gillette razor and a package of blades, so I decided to shave. As I was shaving I kept looking at the razor to see if I had installed a blade. The shave was absolutely so smooth that I couldn't tell I was actually shaving. Later I watched Don shaving with his new razor, and his reaction was similar to mine. He must have checked his blade five times during one shave.

Each package also contained books—books written in English by authors whose names we could recognize and pronounce. My book was *Walden,* by Henry David Thoreau. Crisco had already told me that I couldn't take home the poem I had written in memory of Clarice but that each prisoner could take a book to read while on the plane. I decided to take *Walden* home with me and asked a friend, a civilian named Robert F. Olson, whose eyes were much better than mine, to write the words of my poem at the end of a chapter in the book. He agreed, and he did such a neat job with it that Crisco never even noticed the additional words as he checked for contraband in the bag for the trip home.

I smiled. It seemed symbolic, somehow, that on the very day I was to board the plane, I managed to "win another battle," so to speak, over my captors. But as sweet as that victory was, it paled into insignificance compared to the greatest sensation I ever experienced—the knowledge that I was finally going home. I felt as though I was being born again!

EPILOGUE

On the twenty-seventh of March, 1973, we were turned over to the American authorities at Gia Lam Airport in Hanoi and then flown to Clark Air Force Base in the Philippines. In the C-141 on the way to Clark, the public affairs officer asked me if I would say a few words upon arrival at Clark. It was then that I learned I had been the highest-ranking U.S. Army officer to be a prisoner of war during the Vietnam conflict. While the other men were hugging the nurses, drinking coffee, and smoking cigars, I was busy preparing a few remarks for the crowd awaiting our arrival at Clark.

My first comment was, "Man's most precious possession, second only to life itself, is freedom."

Thirty-two Americans were released that day, including all the American POWs with whom I had had contact at any time and at any place, except Pfc. James E. George, the young man who had retrieved his rifle from the burning helicopter only to be terribly burned. I had sustained the hope all during my imprisonment that James had been given medical treatment and had survived. I now feel certain that he died on the trail that day in February 1968.

The first taste of freedom was absolutely, indescribably delicious. As soon as we had a cursory physical examination we all dined on real, honest-to-goodness American food. But the greatest joy came when I made two phone calls, the first to Anne and the children and the second one to Mom.

After three days of extensive medical examinations and debriefings at Clark, we were flown on to the military hospital in the United States nearest our home. We had stopovers at Hickham Field in Honolulu, at Shephard Air Base in Texas, and at Scott Air Base in Illinois before going on to Bush Field in Augusta, Georgia. It was there at Bush Field on March 30, 1973, that five years of dreams and prayers were answered and I felt Anne in my arms.

David, our oldest son, was standing there in the uniform of a West Point cadet. He was just entering his first year of high school when I left; now he was a cadet in the United States Military Academy and was soon to be an officer in the U.S. Army. He saluted me in what had to be the most gratifying salute of my military career.

"Dad," he said. "I didn't know whether to salute you or hug you."

"Like the soldier you are, you saluted," I replied. Then I smiled. "But a hug would be nice too."

It was.

As I turned from David there stood Debbie, Clifford, Sherri, and Joy, waiting for hugs. Later Joy, who was only twenty months old when I left but now a mature seven-year-old, put her little arms around my neck and said, "Now I have *two* wonderful parents."

It was at that moment that I realized I was finally home.

My mother, who had been very ill at the time of my capture, had been sustained by hope, and she was also waiting for me at the airport.

There was another surprise waiting for me when I finally got to Fort Gordon. Anne had told an interviewer that she thought I would like some watermelon when I got home. The first day of April is a little early for watermelon in Georgia, but there were two waiting for me, presented by the American Watermelon Growers' Association as "a gift from a grateful nation."

As I enjoyed the watermelon, I told Clifford about my vision of him as I contemplated my second escape and how his response had inspired me to proceed with the attempt. He looked at me and said, "I thought you'd do something like that. I'm proud of you."

Of course Anne and I have yet to catch up with all the important information that we each wanted to hear from each other but we did do a pretty good job those first few days and nights. She told me of two incidents which caused me to have flashbacks to Vietnam.

The first flashback was triggered by her remark that at some time after she was advised of my status change from MIA to POW she was told that I had been taken to North Vietnam after my capture. Could this have been a result of my first escape? I'll probably never know for sure the answer to that question.

The second flashback was a result of Anne telling me about her secret meeting with Major Banghasser in May of 1972. I immediately tied the timing of this meeting to my escape from K-49 in March 1972. It was my strong supposition that one of our "friends" in the Hanoi area picked up the information of my escape and forwarded it to our government in Washington.

Perhaps Gene was more correct than I first thought. Perhaps my escape did blow the security of the secret prison, K-49, and this not only precipitated the changing of the guard force there but more importantly, insured our eventual release since they could no longer deny that I was held as a POW. Again, I wish I knew the real truth.

ANNE'S STORY

On March 30, 1973, the glorious event finally arrived. Colonel Gluck escorted us to Augusta, near Fort Gordon, where we were housed in a post guest house until Ben's arrival, scheduled for early that evening. There was a pleasant surprise waiting for us. President and Mrs. Nixon had sent gorgeous white orchids for Mom and me and lavender orchids for the girls. It was something they had done for the families of all returning prisoners of war.

We were transported to the Augusta airport aboard an army bus reserved just for the Purcell family. There were nineteen of Ben's relatives there to meet him. Our wait at the airport was quite lengthy, but finally at dusk the plane arrived and a rousing cheer went up.

The plan of exiting the plane was by rank, so Ben came off first. I stood on the sidelines and watched him as he descended the steps and saluted the commanding generals of the Dwight D. Eisenhower General Hospital and Fort Gordon. Then Ben walked to the cluster of microphones that had been set up for the occasion. Behind the mikes were a multitude of cameramen; video and movie cameras whirred and lights flashed as they took their pictures. My heart was beating rapidly and I was so nervous I found it difficult to stand still. I wanted to laugh and cry at the same time.

Although I didn't do so, I wanted to shout, "Hurry, Ben. Hurry to us. Let us touch you, hold you!"

But no. He talked into the mike forever—at least long enough for me to become concerned for the other families waiting to see and touch their loved ones. I could imagine those families rushing forward, running right over us and Ben to get to the plane.

Suddenly I heard Ben say my name and I could wait no longer. I dashed forward as fast as I could run, right into his arms. As I hugged him I sensed I had interrupted his remarks, so I whispered into his ear, "Are you through?"

"No," he said, as he returned to the mike to finish his statement.

I stood beside him thinking of that first brief moment when he had held me in his arms. I had closed my eyes, and in my mind I had seen two sliding doors come together, sealing off the last five years and leaving us together on this side, poised for a new beginning.

We walked quickly to the sidelines, where once again we were a family united, and that flickering candle in my heart flared into a bright and steady flame.

I could see clearly how the Lord had worked through those years bringing significant people into my life at critical times to provide the help and encouragement I needed to reach this moment.

BEN'S STORY

Following two weeks of intensive medical exams and de-briefings at Fort Gordon, Georgia, I returned to our home in Columbus, where I was greeted by a hundred yellow ribbons around the old oak tree in our front yard. Many friends and neighbors were there to greet us with their welcome signs. One sign in particular summed up our experience. It reads: "Determination to live plus patience to wait equals a joyous reunion for the Purcell family."

Five years is a significant portion of a human lifetime. I could be bitter about those five years, about what it cost my family and me. On the other hand, five years wisely invested can pay off in dividends that can make the rest of a person's time on earth richer and more rewarding.

I like to look at those five years as an investment. It was an investment in our relationship with the Lord. Few people are blessed with the opportunity to meet him on the intimate terms that Anne and I did.

It was an investment in myself. After I was locked in a solitary cell at Bao Cao, I recalled the words of Bishop Fulton J. Sheen: "The man who cannot live with himself cannot live with his fellow man." I have learned to live with myself, and it has enhanced my relationship with my fellow man in more ways than I can count.

It was an investment in my family life. Although we were cautioned about disruptions in family life when we returned, and although, in fact, the wife of one of the pilots of my heli-copter had committed suicide during the long ordeal, the love Anne and I had for each other was strengthened beyond mea-sure. Because those five years were denied us, every moment we now share is more precious.

It was an investment in the experience of courage. Anne had the courage and the strength to go on even through five years of agonizing worry and doubt. I found within myself the courage to survive an ordeal of a magnitude I had only read about before.

Finally, it was an investment in understanding. I have never found it in my heart to hate Armband, Hooknose, Goldtooth, Crisco, or Spit. We were all players upon a larger stage, and each of us had to act according to the roles written for us. That I was able to play my part as well as I did is due to the strength I received from an abiding faith in God and in my country, from the ever-present hope within my heart, and from the matchless love Anne and I had for each other and for the Lord. So then it was these three: faith, hope, and love—but the greatest was love.

The other day I was with a group of people when the friend of one of them happened by. As is customary in such a case, I was introduced and the man held out his hand for a handshake. It was a casual thing for him, this grasping of another man's hand in normal social civility. There was no way he could possibly know that this simple act still can move me to tears of joy.

ABOUT THE AUTHORS

Col. Ben Purcell served in the U.S. Army with distinction for more than thirty years in command and staff positions, from platoon leader to brigade commander, including combat in Korea and Vietnam. He retired from active duty in 1980. His many honors include the Legion of Merit with Oak Leaf Cluster, the Silver Star with Oak Leaf Cluster, and the Purple Heart.

During the years her husband was on active duty, Anne Purcell volunteered her services for many army community projects and worked as a teaching assistant. In 1971, she was chosen as the Fort Benning Military Wife of the Year. Ben and Anne Purcell have been married for over forty years and have raised five children and have two grandchildren. They live in Clarkesville, Georgia, where they operate a Christmas tree farm and lecture extensively on their experiences.